RANA KABBANI

LETTER TO CHRISTENDOM

VIRAGO

Published by VIRAGO PRESS Limited 1989
20–23 Mandela Street, Camden Town, London NW1 0HQ

*A CIP Catalogue record for this title
is available from the British Library*

Printed in Great Britain by
Cox & Wyman Ltd, Reading, Berkshire

For Patrick Seale

CONTENTS

ACKNOWLEDGEMENTS

This book is the result of a talk I was invited to give at English PEN by Lady Antonia Fraser. I owe her an immense debt of gratitude for all the support and encouragement she has shown me since my arrival in London.

The idea for the book came from Ursula Owen. Both she and Lucinda Montefiore engaged me in many stimulating discussions and were my most acerbic critics. I cannot thank them enough for their patience.

I am very grateful to the following for their help at various stages: Hadba Beyhum, Silvia Bottaro, Elizabeth Claridge, Rebecca Fraser, Lisa Jardine, Maha and Sabah Kabbani, Maureen McConville, 'Issam Sabri, Joan Scanlon, and Nabil Sukkar.

FOREWORD

This book is the modest contribution by a woman who had been a sort of underground Muslim before she was forced into the open by the Salman Rushdie affair. Stung by the racial hatred which this affair unleashed, I started to reflect about my own situation as a Muslim in the West. I needed to re-examine my allegiances.

What sort of a Muslim was I? How much of a Westerner had I become? I was caught, it seemed to me, between two tyrannies – that of Ayatollah Khomeini's unacceptable death sentence against a writer who had poked fun at the Prophet Muhammad and, in reaction, the harsh condemnation by the West of what it saw as a barbaric alien culture. Such was the polarisation of these two positions that I began to question whether I could continue living in the West without committing cultural treason – treason, that is, against my own Islamic background. For mine has been a Muslim upbringing and I have tried in this personal memoir to describe what it was like, in the hope that it might illuminate Muslim sensibilities more generally.

In being bold enough to write about myself I am keenly aware of the privileges I enjoyed in a region where the majority is very poor. Yet I believe that what I have in common with less fortunate women from, say, Morocco or Pakistan or Bradford transcends class difference and is greater than what separates us. At first sight I may not conform to the stereotype of a Muslim woman, but my reactions and feelings, my daily habits, my most profound instincts have been indelibly marked by my upbringing. And far from rejecting this upbringing, as I could have done given my early exposure to the West, I have found reason to be grateful for the sustenance it has given me. No doubt many feminists, whether in East or West, have discovered that though liberation is important, there are things rooted in them that matter deeply even if they are not liberating in any simple sense. Contradictions *are* part of everyone's life, especially those living with two cultures.

I am an unashamed champion of my culture, but I am by no means a defender of the many abuses that are committed in the name of Islam. I recognise that there are evident weaknesses and blemishes in Muslim countries, but in this book I have tried to describe what for me is an immensely positive heritage.

I

THE LEGACY OF SLANDER

The Salman Rushdie affair has brought home to me the immense, perhaps unbridgeable, gulf between the world I belong to and the West. No one should suppose that Islam and the West coexisted amicably until Rushdie came along to sour the relationship. On the contrary, there have been tensions between them since the seventh century – that is, since Islam emerged as a political and ideological power able to challenge Christendom.

Am I justified in dredging up what happened in the seventh century? Has this remote history any relevance today? In the West, particularly in the post-war decades, the tendency has been to overlook the past as a direct influence on how we think and feel. Although there is an obsessive preoccupation with the imperial past, children tend to be taught history as something separate from their own existence, as if to suggest that they are products only of individual circumstance and immediate environment. Only the here and now counts. For many Americans and West Europeans, the present is so successful and all-engrossing that it seems to rule out any psychological need to connect with the past.

The groups in Europe who see their present as viscerally linked to their past are those with unsatisfied grievances or threatened identities – for instance the Irish, the Basques, the Corsicans, or the Serbs. I remember being taken round the Kosovo battlefield in Yugoslavia by a Serbian guide who trembled with emotion as he related the defeat of his people – and of Christendom itself – by the Turks on St Vitus's Day, 1389. From that time on, emotions have run high in Serbia on St Vitus's Day and it was perhaps no accident that the Serbian nationalist Gavrilo Princip chose that anniversary in 1914 to assassinate the Archduke Franz-Ferdinand at Sarajevo. Six hundred years after the battle with the Turks, on St Vitus's Day, 1989, a million Serbs went to Kosovo to uphold the Christian message against the enemy from the East – today, alas, represented in their minds by the hapless Albanian Muslim community in their midst. This is a corner of Europe where the contest between Christendom and Islam has a lot of fight left in it.

Muslims understand that history can determine present emotions because that is how they feel themselves. Unlike Westerners, Muslims are for the most part too poor and insecure to afford the luxury of individual feelings: instead, their reactions to events are strongly shaped by communal memories. Easterners have been saddled with history, and it is usually a history of grievance.

Every American child learns that 'In 1492 Columbus sailed the ocean blue', but for most Americans this decisive moment, which saw the emergence of the West as we know it, is little more than a sentimental symbol emptied of political content, not unlike the turkey and pumpkin pie of Thanksgiving which are meant to recall the survival of the pioneers in their first winter on the bountiful 'new' continent. How different for Israeli schoolchildren is the resonance of the Masada story, presented as a metaphor for contemporary psychological survival.

Arab children, too, are taught that their history is indissolubly part of their present. At school they learn the story and share the tears of Boabdil, the last ruler of Muslim Spain, who surrendered the keys of Granada to the Catholic kings in 1492. When his mother chastises him – 'You weep like a woman for what you failed to defend as a man!' – the rebuke is keenly felt, for Arabs are aware that history slipped at that moment from their grasp, setting them on their decline and Christian Europe on its imperial destiny. The loss of Spain is not just a dusty entry in Arab history books but almost a contemporary event, prefiguring more recent catastrophes and in particular the loss of Palestine.

Were Westerners to admit it, they would no doubt recognise that their own attitudes towards Muslims are profoundly marked by half-conscious folk memories of struggle stretching back over the centuries. How else can one explain the peculiar outbursts of anti-Muslim sentiment of, say, a Fay Weldon? In *Sacred Cows*, her contribution to the Rushdie debate, she writes:

> The Koran is food for no-thought. It is not a poem on which a society can be safely or sensibly based. It gives weapons and strength to the thought police – and the thought police are easily set marching, and they frighten . . . I see it as a limited and limiting text when it comes to the comprehension of what I define as God.

And she concludes, with a fine dose of cultural arrogance, 'You can build a decent society around the Bible . . . but the Koran? No.'[1]

Are such rash judgements based on first-hand knowledge of Muslim society? Has Ms Weldon studied Arabic or Islamic history? Is she aware of the context in which the Qur'anic precepts were given? Further on in her text she comments on the demand by British Muslims for their own schools: 'Of course they are not right,' she scolds. 'You cannot, should not, teach a primitive, fear-ridden religion, beat it into children.' Ms Weldon would feel at home in the crowd at Kosovo, for her shrill tone reveals an ancient Christian fear of Muslims which was half banished by Western victories over the last few generations, but still lurks in the cultural subconscious.

Conor Cruise O'Brien has been at one time or another Albert Schweitzer Professor of Humanities at New York University, editor-in-chief of the *Observer*, and a member of the Irish Senate. Yet when given half a chance to let fly at Muslims, the liberal mask slips. 'Muslim society', he wrote confidently in a recent review, looks profoundly repulsive ... It looks repulsive because it is repulsive ... A Westerner who claims to admire Muslim society, while still adhering to Western values, is either a hypocrite or an ignoramus or a bit of both. At the heart of the matter is the Muslim family, an abominable institution.

And in his conclusion he widens his attack: 'Arab and Muslim society is sick, and has been sick for a long time. In the last century, the Arab thinker Jamal al-Afghani wrote: "Every Muslim is sick, and his only remedy is in the Koran." Unfortunately the sickness gets worse the more the remedy is taken.'[2] O'Brien's extravagant sarcasms reveal, perhaps unconsciously, the symptoms of besieged medieval Christendom.

The legacy of prejudice and ignorance is an ancient one.[3] John of Damascus, a Church Father and religious polemicist who died in 754, was the progenitor of a long tradition of Christian ridicule of Muhammad and the Qur'an. Unnerved by Islam's wildfire spread and threatened as an Eastern Christian by its successes, he turned against it the weapons of diatribe which he had used to combat heretics in his own Church. Muhammad, he claimed, was a heretic of a still more dangerous sort who had produced an evil parody of Christianity by cribbing his ideas from a Christian monk.

It was Christian Spain, overrun by Islam, which put about the view that Muhammad was a licentious and worldly schemer, the very antithesis of the pure, otherworldly, self-sacrificial Jesus. Thus took shape the notion of Muhammad as Antichrist which was to become the rallying cry for the Crusades. Indeed, the triumph of the First Crusade gave credence to these prejudices, encouraging still further excesses so that it was not long before a Pope, Innocent III, could portray Muhammad in 1213 as 'the Beast of the Apocalypse'. Such were some of the crude expressions of medieval theological polemic.

Hostility to Islam was not pure hysteria; it was rooted in a real conflict of interest. Islamic armies had destroyed the Christian empire of Byzantium and were beginning to encroach on Europe. The expanding Islamic empire, a rival political system to the small kingdoms and feudal baronies of the West, posed a genuine military threat.

At the same time, Islam as a militant religion posed an ideological challenge to Christianity, considered all the more insidious because Islam accepted some elements of Christian doctrine while rejecting others. Muslims believed in the unity of God, revered Jesus as a prophet whose virgin birth they acknowledged, and held the Bible to be sacred, respecting Jews and Christians as the 'People of the Book'. However, the notions of the Trinity or of Christ's divinity were anathema, as they seemed to offend against the Oneness of God. Muslims could not concede that the Almighty would allow his Messiah to be crucified. The Christian doctrine that man was born sinful and could be redeemed only by the blood of Christ bordered, for them, on pagan belief.

In addition, believing that man needed no intermediary with God, they rejected the whole priestly hierarchy, the practice of confession, and the institutions of monasticism, so dear to the Christian Church. How a Muslim chose to worship God was considered to be a private affair as long as he or she did not offend against the community. Christianity, in contrast, invaded the privacy of a person's inwardness but had little to say about their detailed conduct as social beings, preferring to render unto Caesar the things that were Caesar's. As a result, Christians were perplexed by the Muslim *shari'a*, the body of pragmatic laws for society drawn from the Qur'an and Traditions (sayings and teachings of the Prophet Muhammad), taking it as evidence that Islam was a less spiritual and more worldly religion than their own, and therefore inferior.

Straightforward abuse gave way to a more reasoned hostility as Christian thinkers like Thomas Aquinas and Roger Bacon wrestled with the ideas of Avicenna and other Muslim philosophers when these began to permeate the Western world from the thirteenth century onwards. Bacon urged Christians to study 'unbelief' – that is to say, Islam – in order to rebut it, using in his arguments the very methods of logic which he had learned from Muslim philosophers such as Averroes.

In spite of the increasing sophistication of the attacks, in the West the legacy of these centuries was a profoundly distorted, demonological view of Islam and of its Prophet. In each generation, writer after writer rehashed old fictions about Muhammad so that it became received wisdom that he was an epileptic whose alleged revelations were no more than fits, that he smeared himself with lipstick and drenched himself in perfume to satisfy his intemperate sensuality, that Islam proscribed wine and pork because its founder – almost always referred to as the 'pretender', the 'deceiver', the 'apostate', the 'idolator', or 'Mahound' the Devil himself – had, when in a drunken stupor, been torn apart by swine.

It became intellectually impossible in the West to perceive Islam in any other terms than those of this plainly inimical, even paranoiac, tradition. The caricature of Islam became a central belief of the Christian Church, spreading its poison into secular thought as well. So pervasive was the prejudice that even those scholars, linguists and travellers of the last two or three hundred years who endeavoured to study Islamic society, the so-called Orientalists, often fell victim themselves to the distorting mirror of this tradition.[4] But whereas early detractors of Islam had spoken from ignorance, the Orientalists often used their knowledge of the Qur'an and of Islamic history to reinforce the old discreditable legends.

For example, it is striking that three stories in particular recur time and again in Western writings. The first, already mentioned, is that of Muhammad, described as an ambitious illiterate who is supposed to have learned his religion from an Arian monk, producing a parody of a faith in which the good bits derive from

6

Christianity and the bad from his own imaginings. The second story is that of Zayd, a slave whom Muhammad actually freed, reared as his foster son and married to his own cousin Zaynab, daughter of a noble family, to teach that in Islam all men are equal. But Zaynab and her clan, still influenced by pre-Islamic ideas, were unhappy with an alliance offensive to their pride of lineage. She so taunted her husband as a man unworthy of her that he divorced her, whereupon Muhammad – who felt responsible for her and made a point of marrying widows, slaves or cast-offs to show that such women were not pariahs – wed her. The Orientalist version of this tradition, however, has it that the depraved Muhammad lusted after his daughter-in-law and engineered the breakdown of the marriage for his own satisfaction.

A third story about Muhammad, which has recently been given fresh currency, is the legend of the so-called 'Satanic Verses'. When Muhammad began his ministry in Mecca, around 610, one of his first acts was to condemn idolatry and proclaim that God was One – an unpopular move because the Meccans derived a considerable income from pilgrims who came to pay tribute to pagan gods and goddesses in the Ka'ba, then as now a central place of worship. However – and this is the controversial part – it is alleged that a few years later he rehabilitated three of the goddesses, saying that they had intercessionary powers after all.

That Muhammad related something of this sort before his tribe is claimed by a handful of commentators,[5] but they do not agree on the actual wording of what he is supposed to have said. Moreover, it is probable that this charge was first made by Zoroastrians who penetrated Islam in order to subvert it, and particularly its central monotheistic doctrine. The great majority of reputable commentators deny that the Prophet ever resacrilised the goddesses, and in any event there is no evidence that the 'Satanic Verses' ever appeared anywhere in the Qur'an. This has not prevented Orientalists latching on to the legend as proof that Muhammad was a power-hungry and unprincipled manipulator who, to win support

7

from vested interests in Mecca, was prepared to jettison his most fundamental doctrines. Indeed, this is the view propagated in Salman Rushdie's contentious novel, where Muhammad is portrayed as a businessman with an eye for the main chance.

These stories, and others like them, have been used over the centuries to justify a depiction of the Prophet as plagiarist, libertine and opportunist, a picture which is with us still. It was hoped that a character assassination of Muhammad would discredit and bring down the whole of Islam. The implicit analogy was with Christianity, which is built around the virtuous person of Christ and depends crucially on his redemptive sacrifice. The only way to the Father is through the Son. In Christianity, therefore, to attack Jesus – to imply, for example, that he was a man with human lusts – is to undermine the whole edifice, which perhaps explains the furore over Scorsese's film *The Last Temptation of Christ*. On this model, it was supposed that Islam could be destroyed by destroying the reputation of its Prophet. There is a hint of this approach in the way some Western scholars persist in referring to Muslims as 'Mohammedans'.

There seems little doubt that the long history of denigration and ridicule, fed by Church Fathers, crusading knights, theologians, travellers, oriental scholars and contemporary novelists, is in itself a formidable obstacle to tolerant understanding.

In Britain Rushdie's book brought into the open the frustrations of a Muslim minority for whom the much-vaunted multicultural society was a sham. It felt that its rights were not adequately addressed.[6] Faced by the entrenched majority community, still overwhelmingly Christian in law and in institutions if not in belief, Muslims felt powerless and unprotected. The book-burning in Bradford was something of a desperate attempt to get media attention after less sensationalist protest went unnoticed. Up to this point British Muslims had been largely invisible, but when they resorted to outrageous demonstrations in their attempt to get the government to act against Rushdie's book, they matched the traditional Western image of them, making it easy to label them as primitive fanatics not civilised enough to appreciate the value of free speech.

But their protests changed the landscape. 'Bradford' now has a different resonance, as 'Brixton' acquired in its time. When Keighley, the steep northern town where Charlotte Brontë borrowed books from the public library, erupted into riots, it was plucked out of the English literary past and put squarely in the complicated, multiracial British present.

The Muslim community has raised its voice and its fist. No one likes what it says or the broken, incoherent way in which it is said, but at least everyone listens and wonders what these aliens are about. It was not immediately understood that what Muslims wanted above all was respect and recognition for their religion – indeed, for their identity – after long centuries of abuse. They didn't want to be humiliated any more. They were rejecting the sneering Western tradition and even trying to kill it, throwing it violently back into the faces of their detractors. When, in Ravenna early in 1989, Muslims threatened to blow up Dante's tomb and demanded the banning of the *Divine Comedy*, they were protesting at the way this early secular text of European literature relays medieval Church slanders against Muhammad. Such protest cannot be dismissed as mere religious fanaticism run wild. Rather, it is that for Muslims, cultural and political identity is indissolubly tied to religion, so that to attack the latter is to undermine the former. In this tight bonding of religion and identity, Muslims are more like Jews.

What enrages Muslims today is that the Western tradition which slanders and misrepresents them has lived on long after the winding up of Western empires and the freeing of subject peoples. Western culture remains permeated with anti-Islamic references. Today's media coverage often carries echoes of the medieval polemic. The *People*, a popular Sunday paper, devoted a full page to a photograph of Ayatollah Khomeini's funeral, showing the vast grieving crowd engulfing the body, under the banner headline 'The Mullah's Mad Body-Snatchers'.[7] Western attitudes of cultural contempt are with us still.

Muslims might even argue, with some justice, that twentieth-century scholarship has failed to examine Islam in all its diversity in the calm and objective manner it deserves. Instead, all too often the emphasis is on Islamic violence, terrorism and fanaticism. Much as Western discussion of Communism has, until very recently, been coloured with prejudice and fear, so is discussion of the so-called Islamic threat to Western interests. No doubt the fact that many Islamic countries are also theatres of great political controversy – whether over oil or strategic interests or over such long-running conflicts as the Arab–Israeli dispute or the Gulf War – contributes to the highly coloured way these issues are discussed. Nor, in Muslim eyes, can the West escape the charge of racism, for had Scandinavians or Canadians been Muslim, would the stereotype have been so disagreeable, would the representation have been so disparaging? The world is familiar with the angry and sometimes defensive way Jews react to criticism because of their history of persecution. The clearest thing to emerge from the Rushdie affair is that Islamic anger has, in turn, made its voice heard and become a force to be reckoned with.

What to do about Islam has been a problem for the West from the very beginning. This rival system showed itself to be extraordinarily resistant and indigestible. Over the centuries, attempts to convert Muslims failed and attempts to conquer them proved short-lived. In our own time the West has been more successful in sabotaging Muslim society and fuelling its wars by supplying it with weapons of destruction, but this has not yet resulted in Muslim countries collapsing altogether. If anything, defiance of the West seems to be growing stronger.

From the Muslim side of the divide, the problem looks somewhat different: how to survive culturally and politically in a world still wholly shaped by Western ideas, run by Western technology and dominated by Western power. It is a formidable dilemma made all the more difficult for Muslims to tackle rationally by the overpowering sense of grievance which they can't help feeling because of their experience of being colonised, manipulated and despised. In today's scale of values, a Muslim life seems to weigh a good deal less than a Christian or a Jewish life.

I have come to think that anti-Semitism, endemic in Western culture, has more or less been forced underground. Thankfully and for good historical reasons, it is no longer easy to attack Jews publicly or depict them in fiction as unpleasant caricatures. But these salutary taboos do not extend to Muslims. I would even be so bold as to argue that there has been a transfer of contempt from Jews to Muslims in secular Western culture today. Many Muslims share this fear: indeed, one has written that 'the next time there are gas chambers in Europe, there is no doubt concerning who'll be inside them.'[8]

For a Muslim such as myself the choice, when I first came to live in the West, seemed to be between assimilation and confrontation. Should I sink my identity in my new environment, taking on its colouring and its values, albeit at the risk of being rejected in the end? Or should I resist its influence, shut it out, fight it if necessary, at the risk of finding myself isolated in a ghetto?

I wrestled with the problem, sometimes assimilating and sometimes confronting. I didn't much like doing either. Assimilation made me feel that I was betraying my background, while confrontation made me feel like a fanatic and left me exhausted and embittered. There were many things about the West that I admired and wished to adopt and, equally, many things about Islam that I wanted to cling to. To find a halfway house to inhabit seemed very difficult, seeing that I was the product of two states of thought and feeling, two worlds apparently incapable of meeting on common ground, each a complete system in which everything was interconnected and nothing could be had in isolation from the rest. What I sensed happening in me was the formation of two distinct personalities which, in spite of their visceral relationship, hardly acknowledged each other's existence. Is such schizophrenia the experience of all migrants to a culture not their own, or is it the special predicament of a Muslim in the West? After ten years of unease, I am beginning to feel that a balance has to be struck between my Muslim and Western experience. My need to arrive at such an accommodation is the chief reason for this book.

2

A MUSLIM UPBRINGING

I was born in Damascus thirty-one years ago in a quiet, leafy street named after a stormy revolutionary, Abu Zharr al-Ghafari, an early companion of the Prophet and one of the first Muslims. He had come to live in Syria after Muhammad's death, but the extravagance of the 'Umayyad court outraged him. 'I am amazed', he thundered, 'that the hungry do not rage into the street sword in hand' – a message which made the poor flock to his side. To silence the firebrand, the Caliph sent him into exile, where he died in 652, but his spirit came to rule the place of my childhood and perhaps made me something of a rebel as well.

I was given a Muslim upbringing, a complex package of beliefs and attitudes, some of which I am only today rediscovering in myself. The old adage that Islam is a total religion means that it is not only a theology – belief in God and in the message of his Prophet – but a whole way of living. It affected the way I viewed my parents and the neighbours, determined what we ate and drank, how we washed, how we dressed, how we spoke, how we saw the world – especially the non-Muslim world of the West.

Although I was born in a European-style apartment, home in the imagination of my family remained the traditional Damascene house built around a courtyard from which my parents had moved a few years before. Located in the old quarter of the city and inhabited by countless cousins, aunts and uncles, it was where the extended family had lived for generations. With its blank façade on the street, its secret interior world of fountain and lemon tree, its separate entrances for men and women, it was the classic setting for Muslim family life of all classes. Both my parents grew up in such houses.

As a child my mother played hopscotch in the spacious central courtyard of her grandfather's mansion in Suq Saruja, not far from the 'Street called Straight' in old Damascus. Red pompoms dangled from her socks and the household's Persian cat jumped at them as she hopped from one chalked circle to another. Later in the day, as the heat faded, the jasmine covering the high walls opened its white petals. Water trickled from a bronze spout in the centre of a marble fountain, and the cat, now bored with humans, sat on its polished edge eyeing the darting goldfish. In such places large clans lived together, intermarried and multiplied, quarrelled and supported each other, facing society as an inseparable band. But the pressures of changing times forced them to disperse into smaller, independent families, consisting only of grandparents, parents, children and dependants – rather lonely ménages after the bustling beehives of the older establishments.

In the rush to lay down new roads and accommodate the rapid growth of the capital which started in the 1940s, more than half the ancient city was torn down and hundreds of noble dwellings which had stood for centuries were demolished. Their classical layout can still be found in Andalusia, taken there by 'Abd al-Rahman al-Dakhil, the prince who left Syria in the eighth century to found an Arab dynasty in Spain. But the essence of these houses was not so easily destroyed. In moving to new apartments the Damascenes managed to internalise their vanished abodes, retaining in their nature the formality of the public rooms and the sinuous secretiveness of the secluded passageways.

Old habits die hard. For the first twenty-five years of his life, my father lived in a traditional house. After his bath, crossing the open courtyard from steaming *hammam* to bedroom, he would put on a woollen cap to protect him from the cold. Years later, living in a well-heated modern flat, he remained unconsciously faithful to the old habit and still drew on a woollen cap to step from bathroom to adjacent bedroom – until I laughingly pointed out to him what he was doing. Inside every Muslim, sometimes masked by Western clothes and the trappings of modern life, is another world of habits, values and attitudes not always apparent to the Western observer. The outward appearance, especially when adapted to modern life, can easily be comprehended by foreigners, but the inner self often remains unknown.

In the modern apartments to which they moved, Muslims continued to practise their faith, to perform their ritual ablutions (even when this meant uncomfortably washing their feet in a European-style washbasin), to pray, to abide by the arrangements designed to protect the privacy of women, and, as they did in the old houses, to respect the customs governing the great moments of life – betrothal, marriage, the birth of children, the circumcision of boys, divorce, mourning, as well as fasting, the celebration of religious feasts, and the return home from the pilgrimage.

Islam is regularly singled out as the religion which subordinates women. In reality all three monotheistic religions, Judaism and Christianity as well as Islam, are patriarchal and equally dominated by male establishments. All must be condemned on this score or none. The row over women priests in the Christian Church speaks for itself; nor can the dictates of the Papacy on such matters as birth control, abortion and divorce be interpreted as giving Catholic women much freedom in making their own choices. As for Judaism, it closely resembles Islam in its view of women as lesser beings who are expected to mask their charms and defer to the males of the family, their fathers, husbands and sons.

Of course there are aspects of Islam that do oppress women, and as a feminist one must take issue with them. Indeed, such aspects (for example, the custody or inheritance laws) are the subject of lively debate within Muslim societies and among Muslim women, who are as divided and varied in their opinions as are their Western sisters. But no homogeneous oppression exists, since the interpretation of the religious texts differs widely and since practices that are unthinkable in one Muslim country are often common in another (and this for political, not religious, reasons). In fact, in Islamic society as in the West, the oppression of women is usually more the result of poverty and lack of education and other opportunities than of religion. A poor Muslim woman is more likely to suffer than a rich one.

I am always pained by Western misconceptions about the lives of Muslim women. Western ignorance is often inseparable from a patronising view that insists on seeing us as helpless victims, while hardly distinguishing between the very different cultures we come from. Recently, in London, I was visited by a novelist who had come to talk to me about a Muslim character she wanted to put into her next book. 'How can a feminist like you defend Islam,' she inquired, 'when it advocates female circumcision?' As chance would have it, that same day I read a piece by the historian Marina Warner in which she described Islam as a religion that practises clitoridectomy.[9] Could these two writers not have taken the trouble to discover that this was an African practice which had nothing whatsoever to do with Islam?

We are constantly bombarded with descriptions of the 'terrible plight' of Muslim women allegedly forced into arranged marriages by cruel fathers. These descriptions uphold a false notion that arranged marriages mean lack of choice for the woman.

My sister, when she was eighteen, married in this way. She had spent almost all her life in the West and was hardly distinguishable from a Western teenager. The man she chose from among the suitors presented to her lived in Europe, yet he, like my sister, went home for a marriage partner. Both found it natural and comfortable to go through the traditional steps – just as a Western couple find dating natural and comfortable. Both were more than happy to leave the negotiations about their future to their parents, and within three months – the normal period allowed for the business – they became engaged and were married. At the convent school I attended in Damascus in 1973 the three dozen or so Muslim girls in my class could not conceive of marriage outside the secure framework of arranged betrothals, and for the vast majority of Syrian girls, poor as well as rich, this is still true. They would be aghast if they had to undertake the sometimes desolating search for marriage partners of single people living away from home in Western capitals. No doubt the eclipse of the Church in the West as a meeting-place and a focus of the community explains the great expansion in dating agencies.

Scorned as a poor substitute for romance, these marriage arrangements have as good a chance of succeeding as any other. There is a romantic pretence in the West that things like background, level of education or of culture, money, class and religion are not divisive forces in personal relationships. But precisely because these factors are taken seriously in arranged marriages, bride and groom are in for fewer surprises. They know what to expect and are usually not disappointed, which in marriage is half the battle won.

Western criticism of Muslim family deliberations is perhaps partly tied up with distrust of the very notion of the family. In their efforts to break away from traditional patterns of living, early feminists looked on the family as a suffocating and imprisoning system that had to be totally rejected, but such feelings have evolved. More feminists are choosing to have families of their own ('choosing' here is, of course, the key word) and are discovering how deeply their own identity is determined by their family background – not always in the negative ways they first assumed.

Arranged unions in Muslim societies simply mean that families introduce their sons and daughters to each other as eligible candidates for marriage. Usually the young man's mother and sisters call on the young woman and her female relatives for a preliminary sounding out. If the women get on – and it is they who really decide these matters in the end – the young man and his father are brought along on a second visit to meet the girl and the rest of her family. If the two young people find each other appealing, their parents discuss an engagement which will allow the couple to get to know each other better, usually in a series of family outings or visits and other such chaperoned occasions. These are not only middle-class arrangements; they are observed throughout society.

A Muslim girl cannot be forced to marry against her wishes, although there can be strong pressures, varying from family to family and often the result of economic difficulties. She has the right to reject any partner chosen for her by her family. Before the marriage ceremony the sheikh must ask her if she is entering the marriage of her own free will, and he will not proceed unless he is convinced that she is doing so.

If the engagement goes smoothly and the couple decide they really wish to marry, negotiations over the marriage contract begin, usually conducted by the two sets of parents. These negotiations focus on the size of the dowry, which is paid by the husband to the wife rather than the other way round, as in non-Muslim cultures. I remember how surprised I was to learn that among Christians or Hindus, for example, it was the woman who brought a dowry to her husband.

The Muslim dowry is divided into two parts, with the 'advance' – usually consisting, in middle-class families, of property as well as jewellery and cash – paid to the wife shortly before the consummation of the marriage to give her some financial security and independence. The second part of the dowry, known as the 'later' payment, is made to the wife only if and when her husband divorces her. This solves the problem of alimony and dispenses with the need for further contact or negotiation between the divorced couple. Haggling over the dowry at the start is therefore crucial, as it determines a wife's whole financial future. If agreement is not reached, the marriage simply falls through.

For a Muslim like me, many other Islamic customs are a positive heritage since they deal with things like death, divorce, bereavement of all sorts more humanely than the West does. Far from being rigid and archaic, I believe they have proved adaptable to modern life in Muslim cities.

Mourning rituals, like those surrounding betrothal, marriage and circumcision, provide an understanding of what Islam means to people in their daily lives. To this day in Syria, for example, a woman will try to avoid leaving the house for a full ninety days after the death of her husband, except to visit his grave. The original idea for this prolonged seclusion was that there should be no occasion to dispute the paternity of any child she might bear, but the habit has by and large continued and is part of what is considered socially acceptable, although it too has been adapted to modern life. Women who go out to work, or have no one to shop for them or collect their children from school, are excused. Yet a Syrian woman still wears black for a year after her husband's death, and for the whole of that period she is reluctant to be seen in a restaurant or place of entertainment.

Islamic customs vary widely from country to country, as they do, of course, between Sunnis and Shi'is (the two different sects in Islam). In the Arabian Gulf women mourn their dead for only three days and the colour of the mourning garb is white. Yet what is common to the Muslim world is the absence of that sense of isolation so often felt in the West when a death occurs. In Syria at least, the bereaved is hardly ever left alone in the first week after a death. Preparations for the funeral are attended to by male relatives or by the neighbours. Washers are called in – male or female according to the sex of the deceased – to help the family prepare the body for burial and wrap it in a shroud. Mirrors are turned to the wall and carpets reversed so that the eye is not distracted. Cane chairs for the mourners are rented and a coffee-maker is hired. A sheikh is invited to read aloud from the Qur'an at great length and for days on end, and dervishes are sometimes asked to perform their whirling, mystical dances. For a whole week, members of the family or friends take it in turn to order in, and pay for, special funeral meats to feed the bereaved family and the throng of mourners who descend on them.

For on the actual day of the death, the house is invaded by relatives, friends and neighbours – women sitting with the women of the bereaved family, and men with the men. The women dress in black, dark blue or dark grey and all wear white veils (except for the widow, who wears a black one) and carry prayer beads. Although Islam recommends prayers for the dead and frowns on lamentations, the custom persists and is no doubt a relic of pre-Islamic times. As the body is carried from the house to the graveyard by men in procession to the accompaniment of recitations from the Qur'an, women often break into lamentations. To give voice to their sorrow, upper-class households used to hire the services of wailers, usually poor women who had themselves suffered misfortune. The Prophet disapproved of graveside displays of grief and urged Muslims to bury their dead in unmarked graves so as not to create places of pilgrimage, a practice followed by the strict Wahhabi Muslims of Saudi Arabia. When Faisal, their beloved king, was assassinated in 1974 he was buried in an unmarked desert grave as a reminder that in death all men are equal.

I was nine when my great-uncle, Sa'id al-Ghazzi, a popular former prime minister of Syria, died and I was allowed to attend the mourning ceremonies. He was my grandmother's favourite brother and as we – that is to say my parents, my sister and I – lived in her house, his death affected us all very much. It was the first death in my young life. I noticed that everyone's eyes were swollen from crying. The sheikh who was brought in to intone the

Qur'an was blind, and when he was fed stuffed marrows in tomato sauce, the sauce ran all over his face. The dervishes whirled so vigorously that their skirts stood out from their bodies like hula-hoops. Errand boys from the souk staggered through the house carrying huge brass trays laden with *uzi*, special funeral pasties filled with meat, spiced rice and pistachios which I had not tasted before.

In Damascus a strict mourning ritual is observed for several days after a death. Men and women, each sex at set times, call at the house of the bereaved. They enter the room where the family is seated, stay just long enough to murmur the *fatiha*, the opening chapter of the Qur'an, and file out again with respectfully averted gaze and without another word. These solemn rituals of leave-taking may sound over-elaborate, but they greatly help to distract the bereaved from the loss. And how different they are from the clinical and cursory manner in which the dead are disposed of in the West by 'funeral directors' who, to me at least, often seem little better than tomb-robbers.

Divorce also has its rituals. After my first husband and I divorced, I remember, I travelled to Washington, where my father was the Syrian ambassador. Soon I was out looking for a job. For reasons I could not fathom my father seemed upset, even angry. It was only later, when he blurted it out in an argument with my mother, that I realised he had expected me, even in this foreign setting, to abide by the Muslim custom, the *'ida*, which recommends that a divorced woman should withdraw from the world for three months – for much the same reason as a widow is enjoined to do so. The fact that my father did not make his views clear from the start was itself a pointer to his own uncertainty about the extent to which Islam could be practised in a non-Muslim society. In retrospect, I rather wish he had explained himself more clearly and persuaded me to follow the precept. Instead of recuperating in private for a few weeks, I went out into society before I was emotionally or physically ready and suffered a good deal more as a result.

3

VEILED THREATS

Perhaps one of the most contentious issues for the West, particularly Western women, is the place of the veil in Islamic culture. In the popular mind in the United States and Europe, the veil covering the face is the very symbol of Islam. Yet it is worth recalling that it is of Christian origin, and was adopted by the Arabs only when they conquered Syria in the seventh century in imitation of the social elite they found there and displaced. The veil should not be confused with the Islamic *hijab* which covers a woman's hair, considered sexually attractive and arousing. During the Prophet's lifetime even the *hijab* was worn only by his wives in order to distinguish them from other women. It was later taken on by Muslim women in emulation of these 'Mothers of Islam'. The Qur'an enjoins modesty of apparel, so as not to reveal to men outside her family a woman's hair, her naked limbs or her bosom.

Earlier this century, some relaxation of the rules of modesty crept into Muslim practice here and there, particularly in countries with secular governments. But where change occurred, it met with resistance. When the miniskirt came in and I was allowed to wear one, my paternal grandmother, who never appeared in public without a *hijab*, was aghast. 'The knee is shameful,' she would mutter. And when, aged ten, on the way to the swimming pool, I once ran into the kitchen at home wearing a bathing costume, our aged cook nearly dropped her pot, exclaiming to my mother, 'Aren't you ashamed to let your daughter appear naked in front of men!' When she got no satisfactory reply, she complained to my father.

He calmed her down by reminding her that the Prophet himself had urged Muslims to teach their children, girls and boys alike, to swim, hunt and ride horses.

My paternal grandmother's 'at home' days were occasions when I could observe the rituals of traditional female behaviour. These occasions were the pattern in poor as well as bourgeois homes, where women met together and enjoyed each other's company away from the pressures of their households. The mornings were spent in preparation in my grandmother's house: vats of lemonade were made with grated peel; bowls of custard were laid out to cool in the dark pantry; and everything was cleaned a dozen times: the floors swept and then scrubbed with soap and water, the chests dusted then rubbed with oil to make the marquetry stand out, and the divan covers freshly laundered and starched. Sugared almonds were piled in dishes and *nargilehs* set out for those elderly ladies who smoked and whose disapproving husbands were dead.

The women entered the house by the harem door and, once safely inside the rooms reserved for them, took off their *hijab* and street coats. For the rest of the afternoon that part of the house was strictly out of bounds to men, allowing the guests to relax. Many were wearing their finery, their hair shaped with curling tongs and their eyes ringed with *kohl*. Bare arms and *décolleté* dresses were displayed. Some had brought their unwed daughters, since others had come to find brides for their unmarried sons. The newly betrothed (whether rich or poor) would wear their in-laws' gifts of jewellery for all to admire. Some carried lutes or tambourines to entertain the company while others would sing, dance, or tell stories. The more devout would deliver a religious homily.

My maternal grandmother was a very different story. Her upper-class family wore their religion lightly. Two generations ago, between the two world wars, educated Muslim women like her were flamboyantly tearing off the *hijab*. For maximum publicity, such luminaries of the feminist movement in Egypt as Huda Sha'rawi and Durriya Shafiq dropped their headscarves over the rail of ships or threw them out of the windows of trains as they returned to the Muslim world from Europe. Compared to the secular and scientific West, their own societies seemed stagnant, suffocating and tradition-bound. They had been impressed by the suffragette movement and modelled their own liberation on it.

In the wider political arena, these early Arab feminists agreed with their men that to throw off colonial rule, Western methods had to be adopted because they seemed to hold the key to strength. The most ardent nationalists, those who had suffered most from Western domination, still felt drawn to Western culture.

Across the Arab world, the daughters of this revolutionary generation managed to lead lives not unlike those of Western women of the more affluent classes: going to university, finding jobs in the professions, marrying for love, and bringing up their own families in the modern way. Western fashions were assiduously followed: the New Look was as much 'in' in Damascus as it was in Paris. In the courtyards of the old houses, upper-class men and women danced to the latest tangos and foxtrots on the gramophone; while Western art was admired and studied, influencing style as much as it did in Europe.

When my parents got married in 1956, 'Cubist' furniture was all the rage, so to accommodate their voguish bedroom suite – side tables shaped like Braque guitars and Picasso motifs on the curtains – they threw out (to their later regret) the traditional furnishings of damasked brocade and the bridal chests inlaid with mother-of-pearl.

These trends grew out of a new post-war prosperity, out of the emergence of an educated middle class, out of a widely shared hope that the revolutionary upheavals then shaking the region would lead to political renewal with greater popular participation. Nasser was the hero of the hour. Whenever he spoke, people across the Arab world would be glued to their radios, and when he nationalised the Suez Canal in 1956, crowds ran shouting with excitement into the streets in a spontaneous celebration of the new era.

There was a sense that the whole 'Third World' was awakening and that it had a future which it would fashion itself. Nasser was one of a pantheon which included Nehru, Nkruma, Sukarno – proud leaders who for the first time represented the interests and aspirations of their people. This was the heyday of nationalism. Algeria's eight-year war of independence against France, a classic armed struggle against colonial rule, aroused enormous passions.

One of the heroines of this struggle was Jamila Bouhired, who had been tortured and scarred by her French captors but had inspired a whole generation of Algerian women to become freedom fighters in the war of a 'million martyrs'. In the early sixties, when the war was over, she paid an official visit to Kuwait, where the Minister of Education and a party of veiled women teachers waited to receive her at the airport. She appeared at the door of the plane – with her hair uncovered. Not wishing to embarrass her, and no doubt infected by the spirit of the times, the Minister turned to the teachers and commanded: 'Quick, take off your *hijab*!'

Much has changed today. It would be inconceivable for an official in a Muslim country to order women to remove their *hijab* without starting a riot. This is not only because of the rise of fundamentalism; it is primarily because the *hijab* is no longer seen as a symbol of an archaic tradition. Rather, it has become a striking affirmation of identity – religious, cultural and political – reflecting the more radical feelings that now prevail.

The adoption of the *hijab* by educated and politicised young women, often from secular families, has in the 1980s become an inescapable phenomenon of life in most Muslim cities. There are many reasons for this, but above all it reflects the disillusion of this generation with the achievements of its elders. In the Arab world, independence proved an immense disappointment. No new social order founded on justice was created: instead, corruption and repression ruled. Defeat in war led to the loss of yet more lives and land. Despite Arab rhetoric Israeli hegemony, propped up by the West, remained unchallenged. 'Third World' solidarity collapsed. In Arabia and the Gulf, the very areas where oil wealth in independent Arab hands could have made a difference, Western interests rather than Arab aspirations seemed to prevail. Western products of all sorts, cultural as well as material, flooded the marketplace.

Responding to these setbacks, Muslim feminists no longer choose to model themselves on their Western sisters. The over-permissive West – which they now perceive, perhaps crudely, as exploitive of women, as plagued by drugs and AIDS, and as indifferent to the sufferings of the rest of the world – is to them a less attractive place than it seemed to their grandmothers. At the risk of reiterating what has now become a cliché, it must also be said that the issues which concern them are not those of Western feminists. In the late 1970s a conference was held in Scandinavia on International Women's Day. Among the Arabs present was the Palestinian guerrilla fighter Fatima Barnawi, who had spent long years in Israeli jails, was tortured, and had been forced to watch her father being tortured when no information could be extracted from her. I recall her bewilderment when, newly arrived at the conference, she was exposed to hour-long speeches by European feminists on lesbian rights. Although the importance of debates about sexuality in the context of Western feminism should not be underestimated, the political exigencies of survival in the Middle East could not help but make these issues seem a luxury.

When Arabs today view their society – and much the same could be said for all Muslims – they see a travesty of modernism, neither genuinely Western nor properly Eastern, and certainly not satisfactory. The frenzy of Islamic revivalism must surely be a reaction to this state of affairs. The women who decide to put on the *hijab*, that flag of Islamic commitment, are not retreating from ground won by their grandmothers. Just as it was a political choice fifty years ago to remove the *hijab*, a choice freely made and of great consequence, so the decision today to put it on again is equally momentous and equally political.

These women are not withdrawing to an archaic past, nor do they wish to stay demurely at home. Most often they are professional women, doctors, teachers, pharmacists and lawyers. Politically, they are activists – a sort of Muslim Sisterhood not unlike the Muslim Brotherhood of male militants, but unconnected with it. The wearing of Islamic dress gives these women greater rather than less freedom and mobility, for in such austere garb and with the mentality that accompanies it, they are much less likely to be closely monitored by their families.

Wearing the *hijab* can be a liberation, freeing women from being sexual objects, releasing them from the trap of Western dress and the dictates of Western fashion. Just as feminists in the West have reflected on the connection between 'feminine' clothes and female oppression, so Muslim feminists reject the outward symbols of sexual allure. In favour of the *hijab* it can be said that by distancing its wearer from the world, it enriches spiritual life, grants freedom from material preoccupations, and erases class differences by expressing solidarity with others in the same uniform. Since all women look the same in it, it is a most effective equaliser, and since it camouflages rich clothing, it is in keeping with the Islamic injunction against ostentation. The long dull coat usually worn with the *hijab* is of similar significance and may be compared with the dun-coloured cloak favoured in Renaissance Florence after the passing of the anti-luxury laws.

I have had occasion to observe the *hijab* phenomenon closely because my own cousin, Lama, took to it at the age of sixteen. Her grandmother, the wife of a prime minister of Syria in the 1950s, had thrown it off in her youth. Lama's mother studied law at university, practised at the Bar, and was the first woman in Syria to run a television talk show. She was an attractive young woman with a successful career, who had married the man she loved and was independent, liberated and Westernised in the tradition of the women in her family. Lama's decision was therefore met with considerable shock and disapproval – all the more so when it became apparent that for my cousin, the wearing of the *hijab* meant commitment to a certain form of Islamic activism. Gradually the family adapted to what she had become, but it was always intriguing to visit them and find one daughter dressed like an Islamic nun, her head tied in a scarf, wearing opaque stockings and a long-sleeved garment even in midsummer, with nothing showing but her face and hands, while her two sisters were barebacked in sundresses.

Some practical advantage may be derived from the *hijab*. Western feminists are familiar with the notion of a supportive group of friends, acquaintances and contacts – a female alternative to the exclusive 'old boy' network – and so it is with their Muslim sisters. In most Muslim countries – in Morocco, Algeria, Libya, Tunisia, Egypt, Sudan and Nigeria; in Jordan; in the occupied West Bank and Gaza; in Lebanon and Syria; in the Gulf; in Turkey, Iran, Afghanistan and Pakistan; in Malaysia and Indonesia – something like a women's underground is taking shape, providing an alternative to the apparatus of power and influence which in all these countries belongs to the state and to those most closely associated with it.

Women drawn into this underground are, on the whole, those who have received an education and made their way in life. They are encouraged by friends who are committed Muslims to adopt the *hijab* if they have not already done so. They meet at social gatherings at which something like cells are formed. Soon women discover that this network can provide real advantages – one of its members knows how to obtain a supply of scarce medicines, another can find places for children at an over-subscribed school, a third has a high-placed contact in a ministry. Such connections are extremely useful in developing countries, where life is always something of a struggle and a push by a person of influence is usually necessary to get things done. The network provides an informal matchmaking service, finding husbands for its unmarried members, and also works as a therapeutic group where women can talk about their personal problems and get comfort and advice.

Undoubtedly such coteries can be tainted by fanaticism, by a holier-than-thou exclusiveness, by a blinkered approach to life. Belonging to a Sisterhood and sharing the faith can be attractive but it can also be imprisoning, limiting one's choices on every level. Viewed from the outside such zealotry can be distasteful, as fanaticism is in all religions. But the anger and frustration which fuel it should not be underestimated.

To the secular Western mind, displays of religious fervour by veiled women – but especially by heavily bearded men of dark skin – are always incomprehensible, disagreeable, even frightening. The spectacle of Muslims in large numbers, demonstrating, shaking their fists, clinging passionately to their religion, renouncing the West, arouses understandable anxiety and a defensive instinct. But it is as well to remember that the threatening crowd often itself feels threatened, and seeks in religious fervour a haven from a hostile world. Loyalty to a creed which bonds them together makes Muslims feel politically less vulnerable, particularly at a time when Arab unity, say, or 'Third World' solidarity, has been revealed as bankrupt. There is of course a real conflict which cannot be disguised between mob passions and the Western ideal of individualism, with its rights and freedoms. But beyond this philosophical conflict there is another, more real to Muslims, between a dominating West and a still struggling East. Political and economic frustrations have led to an often worrying increase in religious 'fundamentalism' all over the Muslim world.

Among Arab countries, Tunisia is generally thought to be the one which has perhaps gone furthest down the secular road and where women's rights have been most protected. In the early 1960s Bourguiba, then the pragmatist of Arab politics, tried to jolt his countrymen out of their traditions, which he felt were a brake on progress. He would single out a woman in a crowd and enjoin her to remove her 'ridiculous' veil. During Ramadan he once downed a glass of orange juice in public, arguing that in a whole month of fasting no one could possibly put in a good day's work. Underpinned by legal codes based on Western models, such views caused secularism to bite deep into Tunisian life.

Yet two decades later, and in the last years of Bourguiba's rule, an Islamic political movement emerged as the most powerful challenger of the system he had created. Indeed, Tunisia provides an example of a phenomenon that is spreading not only throughout North Africa but across the entire Muslim world. In neighbouring Algeria, the bread riots that convulsed the country in 1988 and forced the government into reforms had a flavour of the fearlessness inspired by religion. Severe economic hardship has made people turn to God when they despair of salvation from their rulers.

Not long after Bourguiba's removal from office in 1988, a curious incident occurred which seemed to throw light on the feelings of the common people. Saudi Arabia sent Tunisia a travelling exhibition on the pilgrimage to Mecca which included a cardboard model of the Ka'ba, the massive granite cube which stands at the centre of the Great Mosque and has been the focal point of Islam since its foundation. The exhibition produced scenes close to mass hysteria. People queued overnight with their children to get in. The old went in the hope of dying there – as they do to Mecca itself. The place was so crowded and the exits were so congested that a number of women actually gave birth on the spot. People wept with religious fervour, as they do on the real pilgrimage. And on leaving the exhibition, they congratulated each other as though they had actually performed the *hajj*.

4

WORDS AND DEEDS

During my childhood the Qur'an was central to our lives. My grandmother had her father's manuscript copy on a wooden pedestal next to her bed: it was her most prized possession. I often looked up at it when I was invited into her room, although I was careful never to touch it.

I was seven when my mother asked my cousin Bassam, a studious and devout boy four years my senior, to teach me the opening chapter of the Qur'an, known as the *fatiha*. She thought it best, against conventional wisdom, to have a young member of the family rather than an adult instruct me in this important first lesson. She wanted to make it as pleasurable and as unthreatening as possible, for she no doubt sensed that it would affect my view of religion for the rest of my life. I had spent the afternoon playing Scrabble for Juniors with Bassam and his brother and I thought the lesson would be a continuation of our word games, which I had very much enjoyed.

We went into the small sitting-room, where the green jalousies had been lowered against the afternoon sun. I sat swinging my legs and giggling, but Bassam very solemnly told me not to be so childish, for I was about to be taught something more important than anything else I knew, more important than anything I would ever learn, something I should treasure in my mind for ever. I was impressed by the change that came over him, by the grave manner in which he spoke and, determined not to be outdone, sat very still and made a great effort to concentrate.

Bassam recited the *fatiha* very slowly and carefully. He then repeated the first sentence on its own and asked me to say it after him until I had committed it to memory. He did not explain it to me; nor did I, in my usual inquisitive way, ask him about the meaning of the various words. There seemed to be a tacit agreement between us that I would first learn it by heart and then be told what it meant – preferably by someone more knowledgeable than himself.

When my cousin was certain that I could say the whole *fatiha* without making a single mistake he allowed me to go in search of my mother, who was sitting just outside the room on the veranda (where she had probably overheard the whole of our exchange).

'I know it all!' I exclaimed excitedly. 'Shall I say it for you?' My mother nodded, and I began to recite:

> In the name of God, the Merciful, the Compassionate.
> Praise be to God, the Lord of all Being,
> the Most Merciful, the Most Compassionate,
> the King of the Day of Judgement.
> Thee only do we worship, and to Thee do we pray for succour.
> Guide us to the straight path,
> the path of those whom Thou hast blessed,
> not of those against whom Thou art wrathful,
> nor of those who go astray.

My mother hugged me hard after I had finished, and told me how proud she was that I had reached the age of reason. 'Now you are old enough to distinguish between good and evil,' she said, 'and you must try and conduct yourself in a way that will please God. Whisper the *fatiha* to yourself when you are frightened, when you feel sad or discouraged, and it will help you.'

Every Thursday evening after that, my father would choose a passage from the Qur'an for us to read together. He would explain it to me at length, often recounting incidents from the life of the Prophet to illustrate a point or drive home a lesson. He would make me copy out the passage in my notebook, then look at his watch and say, 'You have forty minutes to learn this. I'll call you to recite it when your time is up.'

How well I remember those winter evenings! I would sit in the cold salon with the stove unlit in order not to get too sleepy, and listen to the voices coming from the cosy sitting-room where my family was gathered. The smell of roasting chestnuts would reach me from across the dark hall, and I would steel myself to my task. Often my eye would wander to the library shelves, with their rows of books in English and French, and I would take down my copy of *Jane Eyre* and read a few sentences. But time would be running short, and I would begin my memorisation as soon as I heard the clock on the wall strike the quarter hour. After the first three difficult lines the text would suddenly become accessible and lovely, and I forgot about everything but the words in front of me.

Those hours spent studying the Qur'an taught me a love of language, but the verses I learned as a child were unrecognisable when I read them in an English translation many years later. I could not share their beauty with anyone I knew in the West, for the Qur'an becomes prosaic and even incomprehensible in any tongue but its own: indeed, it says of itself that it was handed down from God as an 'Arabic Qur'an', as though conscious of its own indivisibility from the language in which it was communicated. I firmly believe that the work cannot be translated. A Muslim reading the Qur'an in Arabic and a non-Muslim reading it in translation are simply not reading the same book. Perhaps some small idea of an Arab's feeling for the Qur'an can be gained by considering the English people's reverence, felt even by atheists, for the beauty of the language of the King James Bible. But I think the problem is deeper than the untranslateability of a work of art and concerns Arabic itself, which seems to resist transfer into other languages. I have never come across a successful translation of an Arabic poem, or even of an Arabic novel – let alone of the Qur'an. It seems that our texts are destined to remain only semi-comprehensible to those who read them in translation.

I feel for non-Arabic-speaking Muslims who learn the Qur'an by rote without being able to understand it fully or appreciate its power. Even though their faith cannot be questioned, they remain at a disadvantage, for they can apprehend this linguistic triumph only through the screen of imperfect interpretation. As for non-Muslims who have not studied Arabic, they are, it seems to me, unable to comprehend what the Qur'an says. It remains for them a silent text, and their attempts to analyse it can hardly amount to much.

The impact of the Qur'an on those who hear it in Arabic can be illustrated by the story of 'Umar ibn al-Khattab, a warrior from Muhammad's own tribe, the Quraysh, and one of his fiercest enemies. Tradition has it that 'Umar stormed in a rage into his sister's house when he learned that she and her husband had converted to the new religion. The Qur'an, against which he had fought so hard, was being recited in the next room. He stopped to listen and, unable to resist its power, embraced Islam on the spot – becoming, some years after Muhammad's death, one of the most judicious leaders of the Muslim community.

Since the Qur'an is the sole miracle that Muslims believe in (no less believable than Jesus rising from the grave or walking on water) they accept 'Umar's sudden conversion on hearing the word of God, just as Christians accept Saul's conversion on the road to Damascus. On Fridays, not far from the 'Street called Straight', where a God-fearing Paul was born of a hard-hearted Saul, we would wake up to the smell of the *harira* that my father always made for us on sabbath mornings. I can see him now in that vanished kitchen, standing before a stove and stirring flour and butter, sugar and water, until they turned into the golden drink that was thought to be a cure for ills of all sorts, chesty cough and heartbreak among them.

As we sipped the sweet hot brew, my father would recount the Caliph 'Umar's adventures (stories which his father had once told him; stories which, years later, he would tell his grandchildren in other kitchens in Europe and America). The *harira* tale used to be my favourite, associated with the breakfast he made us.

Every evening, under the cover of darkness, the Caliph 'Umar, 'Prince of the Believers', would slip away from his abode and, disguised in a ragged cloak, wander through the backstreets of the city to see for himself how the Muslims were faring. One bitter night he chanced upon a group of figures huddled together. Approaching closer, he distinguished a woman surrounded by her moaning children. 'Hush, my babies,' 'Umar heard her say, 'your mama is making your supper.' But on coming closer still and peering into the pot, he saw that it contained nothing but pebbles and water. The woman looked up at the ragged stranger and said in a miserable whisper, 'May God have mercy on those with empty stomachs.' Distraught at this spectacle, the Caliph murmured 'Amen' and hurried off to fetch some provisions. Soon he returned with a sackful, quickly lit the fire, threw out the stones from the pot and began to brew some *harira*, stirring it round and round until it was good and hot and thickened. Ladling it out to the mother and her children, he then gave them bread and meat and fruit – and later somewhere to live, money to spend, and so on to the happy ending.

Even as very young children my sister and I were taught that food was sacred – the very word for food, *na'ma*, meant 'blessing', the gift of God – and that to waste it was a crime. We were forbidden to leave anything on our plate, not because it was bad manners but because food was precious and others were in need. If we saw a piece of bread lying in the street, we had to pick it up, kiss it and touch our forehead with it, and then put it out of harm's way where it would not be trodden on. When my Uncle Nizar was posted to London as a diplomat, his old mother, a pious lady, came to visit him. At a reception she attended, she noticed that one of the guests had dropped a cocktail snack. She stooped down, picked the morsel off the carpet, kissed it and touched her forehead with it, and then replaced it on the plate of the bewildered guest.

When food was cooked in the house, it was the custom in my childhood for a portion to be sent to the neighbours – and I was often the one to deliver it – because it wasn't considered seemly that they should smell the dish cooking and not be able to taste it. To this day, food gets passed up and down the stairways of apartment blocks. In those days rich and poor lived much more side by side than they do today, and this was true for all the buildings in the street where I was born. The poor lived in the basement or right at the top in a couple of rooms on the roof, while the better-off inhabited the floors in between. Rich and poor children of all classes played together. Whatever their income or status, all the families socialised and helped each other out. Such easy intermingling of classes was the traditional pattern of Islamic society, endorsed by the Prophet himself, who declared: the best among you is not the richest but the most pious. Invocations of God, reminders of the Prophet's teaching, and phrases of piety are not, in Islamic society, confined to holy days and prayer times but are woven into every conversation from the day's first 'good morning' to its last 'good night', leaving an imprint on attitudes and manners that cannot be denied.

Only in recent years, with the breakdown of Muslim values and the remodelling of Muslim cities on Western lines, have new quarters sprung up, inhabited exclusively by the better-off. The segregation which followed has denatured and impoverished social life. In my childhood, the festival marking the end of Ramadan, the annual fast – the Muslim 'Easter' – was a joyous occasion when rich and poor neighbours celebrated the '*Id* together on an equal footing. Today, in the smart apartment buildings of the rich, the local errand boys, the doormen and the garbage collectors will ring the doorbell for their annual tip, much as they do in the West, and not be invited in. Regrettably, it is also true that the celebration of Islamic festivals has become as senseless and perverse as the celebration of Christmas in the West: rampant consumerism, ostentatious displays of wealth from which the poor are shut out – in fact, the very antithesis of the spirit of these religious moments.

Learning to distinguish between *halal* and *haram*, between what is allowed and what is forbidden, and also between *tahir* and *nijis*, between what is clean and what is unclean, lies at the root of a Muslim upbringing. In my own case, these two sets of opposites have penetrated the very fibre of my being, dictating a whole range of behaviour – from my dislike of having dogs in the house to my horror of mice, my aversion to the smell of bacon (dogs, mice and pigs are considered unclean by Muslims), my compulsive cleaning and washing and my strict views on household management. The Muslim ethic is more concrete than the Christian: it is as concerned with practical matters as with abstract principles.

Twice every year I am seized by an uncontrollable urge to spring-clean my house, an instinct so strong that I wake up in the middle of the night and think about how to plan it. After the feast that marks the end of Ramadan, and again six months later, my mother used to wash the carpets, the floors, the walls, the ceiling, the shutters, the upholstery covers and all the bedding with soap and water. To help with this massive twice-yearly ritual, five or six women were brought in. Among the poor, five or six women will help each other and work together, for the six-monthly scouring happens in all homes. Modern flats in Damascus are often built with a drain in a corner of each room to cater to the need of Muslim housewives to throw buckets of water over the tiled floors. My grandmother, who made spring-cleaning a daily task, even used to soap the leaves of the lemon trees in her courtyard in old Damascus. My grandfather would object that it was pointless work seeing that it was about to rain, to which she would reply: 'God forbid that rain should fall on dirt.'

The obsession with washing is related in Muslim minds to respect for God, on the argument that in caring for the body, one is paying tribute to its maker. As with the Quakers, physical cleanliness is thought to be a passport to spiritual purity. Washing, ordering and tidying are also ways of overcoming chaos, which Muslims believe is the work of the Devil. No doubt the fact that many Muslims live in countries that are hot, crowded and arid, and where the street is often dirty, has led them to prize cool and clean houses and to consider water the most precious of commodities. It is also a commodity which belongs to everyone. In Damascus, for example, you can go into a shop and, without saying a word to anyone, drink or wash from a tap. Every building has a tap somewhere out in front, on the model of the public drinking fountain on every street in the old quarters, and anyone can draw water from it without asking permission, a mode of behaviour quite unknown in the West. My mother, strolling down a boulevard in Paris one day, had eaten a sticky cake. She saw a gardener watering plants and approached to rinse her fingers under his hose. '*Non, Madame,*' he said. '*L'eau appartient au propriétaire.*'

To Muslims, the ideal house has an inner courtyard graced by a splashing fountain – the epitome of this is the Alhambra palace in Granada. The Muslims in Andalusia used to say that there is music in the sound of flowing water, in the laughter of the beloved – and in the jingle of coins, for, incidentally, there is nothing reprehensible about money in Islam. The Qur'an says that children and money are the gems of worldly life, a very different notion from the New Testament's denigration of earthly riches or the 'filthy lucre' of popular Western parlance. In the Muslim ethic, wealth can and should be used to feed the poor, to fund education, to build mosques and to perform the pilgrimage to Mecca – all activities which find favour in God's sight. If one has all this to one's credit, there is no guilt in having a good time with the rest of one's money.

The religious texts say that cleanliness is next to holiness and that one should not pray to God or touch the Qur'an unless one's body is clean. When I was about to leave for England, my great-aunt expressed concern: 'I'm told that whole families sit in the same bath water and don't rinse themselves,' she said. According to Muslims, rinsing away impurities is the only way to true cleanliness. I am still surprised at the often casual way in which the British wash their dishes, for a Muslim upbringing enjoins that they must be rinsed back and front seven times.

From an early age Muslim children are taught the great importance of washing their private parts with soap and water every time they use the lavatory, functions for which European bathrooms are not always designed. My sister, who lives in New York, was telephoned by her puzzled American neighbour about her little boy, aged three, who had gone over to their house to play. He was refusing to get down from the lavatory, demanding that his bottom first be washed with soap and water. Lavatory paper alone would not satisfy him.

To Western readers such a degree of refinement may seem a badge of the middle class, but the regime of personal hygiene is observed by anyone who can afford – or has access to – water. Beside every mosque is a washroom or, at the very least, a fountain in the courtyard where the faithful perform their ablutions. A common sight throughout the Muslim world is of men splashing about before going in to pray. This is because Islam lays down a strict ritual of washing before prayer: water must pass over hands, elbows, feet, face, ears, neck – and, of course, over the more private parts. These ablutions must be done before the first of the five daily prayers, and need to be repeated before the subsequent prayers if, in the meantime, one has had sex, dirtied oneself unduly at work, or used the bathroom. Even breaking wind demands a new bout of washing.

For both men and women, washing before and after sex is essential. Women are also taught that it is 'cleaner' to remove all bodily hair, a painful ritual which involves spreading a paste of boiled sugar on the skin and then tearing it off. A woman's menstrual period is considered an unclean state in which fasting, prayer, reading the Qur'an or visiting a mosque are not allowed. The end of a period is marked by elaborate washing accompanied by invocations to recover the body's purity. Boys are circumcised because the foreskin is thought to be a trap for dirt.

These habits of cleanliness have, over the years, become part of a way of life. Behind all this washing is the wish to emulate the Prophet who, according to Tradition, was clean, sweet-smelling, fastidious and immaculately though simply dressed. Out of respect for fellow Muslims, he is said to have discouraged people from attending the Mosque if they had just eaten onions or garlic. 'Cleanliness', he said, 'is part of faith.'

For my part I do not consider the Muslim preoccupation with cleanliness oppressive or sexist, although I can see that it might seem so to a Western sensibility. However, it must be acknowledged that this preoccupation with cleanliness can sometimes degenerate into xenophobia. At a hairdresser's in Damascus I overheard an orthodox Muslim woman say to the manageress: 'It's just as well you got rid of that Armenian girl who shampooed my hair last time. I'm sure her hands weren't clean . . .' – an expression of the Muslim suspicion that Christians do not wash as scrupulously as they should.

Of course, the prejudice works both ways: Christians are equally convinced that it is Muslims who are dirty. My grandfather, Tawfiq Kabbani, who had fought the French in Syria and been imprisoned by them, still admired their civilisation enough to send my father to study law at the Sorbonne. He managed to separate in his mind the political system that oppressed him from the culture he admired, a separation more difficult to sustain today because we are more aware of the deep complicity between culture and power. When my father, a fanatical washer descended from a long line of fanatical washers, arrived in Paris from Damascus as a student in a starched shirt and with a year's supply of Aleppo soap in his trunk, he spent his first night at an insalubrious hotel on the Left Bank. Exhausted from his journey, he sat down in the dingy lobby, closed his eyes and rested the back of his head against the wall, only to be roused by a shout from the evil-smelling concierge: 'Take your head off my wallpaper, you'll soil it!'

5

WESTWARD HO!

My Muslim upbringing was interrupted by a number of forays into Western culture occasioned by my father's diplomatic postings abroad. On these trips outside Syria I was confronted with values with which I neither could nor wanted to conform – so from an early age I felt I had to lead a double life: one at home, another at school. These lives were not reconcilable and this, in a small way, was my first introduction to the wider clash between Islam and the West. As a Muslim girl hemmed in by all sorts of restrictions – unable, for example, to go to parties or to have boyfriends – I found myself an outsider. To bolster my self-respect, to avoid being looked down upon, I worked hard and did well at school. If there were any prize going, I felt I had to win it, and usually did. It was my way of overcoming a sense of being different. Later on, at university in America, I noticed that the students who won the best grades tended to be foreigners like myself. At lectures we all sat in the front row, all driven by the same urge to succeed and show the natives that we were as good as they were, if not better.

The first foray abroad was to New York City when I was five, and the first shock was to find myself alone with my father and mother, who had not until then been the focus of my life. The people with whom I had spent all my time were my grandmother and two retainers, Fatima the cook and Mutiya, who looked after me. Then there was my great-aunt, who lived next door, and my cousins, who were always in the house. In Damascus, the school I went to was across the street from our house – from my classroom window I could see my grandmother smoking a cigarette on her balcony as she pruned the roses – and next door to the school was the hospital where I was born.

In New York it was sudden isolation, my first taste of living within a nuclear family in an anonymous urban environment. I wasn't alone in feeling a sense of desolation. I remember that when the boxes containing our things were carried into the apartment in Sutton Place where we were to live, my mother sat down on one of them and burst into tears. I had never seen her cry before, no doubt because in an extended family she would have had someone to comfort her before she broke down. Just as it was the first time I found myself alone with my mother, so it was the first time she had been separated from hers.

Feeling homesick, she put a record of Arabic music on the new gramophone my father had bought her, and played it rather loud. Soon there was a knock on the door, and a neighbour appeared. 'Is that Umm Kalthum you are playing?' she asked, as my mother hastened to turn down the sound. It emerged that our neighbour had lived in Lebanon, recognised the music, and had come to befriend us. By this stroke of luck, isolation in the big alien city became bearable for both of us, since our neighbour happened to have a daughter my age.

Once enrolled at school, I discovered to my surprise that several of the girls in my class looked very like the girls I had known in Syria, and they became my friends. As I did not speak much English, communication was limited, but when we went down to the canteen for lunch, like me they did not eat pork and were allowed two portions of dessert instead. One day the principal came into the class and asked a question I could not catch. Seeing my friends raise their hands, I did so as well. But what she had said was, 'Who in the class is Jewish?' And just as I had got my religion wrong, so to my teacher's amusement, when it came to writing English, I started off, as with Arabic, from right to left.

Another early lesson was about the perils of living in Manhattan. I remember my father, looking very grave, unfolding a newspaper to show me the picture of a little girl who had been attacked in Central Park (where I was often taken for walks) and then stabbed in the stomach. Like me, she was six. 'This is a dangerous country,' he said. 'You have to be careful whom you talk to and where you play.' A few days later I came back from school to find my mother telephoning my father at the office in great distress to say that she had had enough and wanted to return home. A woman had been killed two floors up in our apartment block. She had ordered some vegetables from the nearby shop and her assailant, pretending to be the delivery boy, got her to open the door. What was most shocking to my mother was that when she screamed, no one had come to help her. Almost as unnerving for my mother was the discovery that some call girls were running a high-class brothel in the apartment across the landing. All this was very different from the gentle, demure, tightly knit world she had been used to in Damascus.

At the age of nine my great friend was Gilda, a Jewish princess in embryo, always tanned from expensive holidays. She lived with her divorced mother, of whom she was an almost identical miniature version, and the appearance of both proclaimed to the world that they were secular members of the New York Jewish *beau monde*. They lived in a luxurious penthouse round the corner, decorated in different shades of white. On my visits to her apartment, her mother was either on the phone or lounging about in a turban and a see-through negligee, giving me my first glimpse of a grown-up naked female body. Ash from her cigarette, in a long diamanté holder, would fall on the white carpet.

In Damascus there was greater prudery and much more covering up, even between members of the same family. It may have had something to do with people of different generations inhabiting the same quarters, together with domestics, like in a Victorian household, so that my mother, for example, never ventured outside her bedroom except in a dressing-gown. But Gilda's mother was different. I learned that she slept naked with the man who soon became Gilda's stepfather, and Gilda was allowed into their bedroom. Indeed, the three of them shared baths together, a concept that I could barely take in.

But what amazed me equally was that Gilda's mother was forever rearranging the furniture. The white grand piano would reappear in quite different settings. In my grandmother's house nothing ever changed place, nor had done since she moved in. Each room had a function and each piece of furniture its proper place. Every middle-class salon in Damascus was exactly alike, with the same Persian carpet in the same spot, the same mother-of-pearl inlaid pieces, the same Chinese jardinières, the same ostrich eggs decorated in ink with verses from the Qur'an, the same opaline vases in marquetry cabinets. Children were not allowed in the room except on special occasions, nor was it used by the family. It was reserved for guests. The idea of living in the salon and of moving things about simply for pleasure did not exist. Only at the time of the biannual spring-clean was the furniture displaced before being put back as before. We used to tease my grandmother when she complained that new maids 'didn't know how to put things in their place'.

In New York the parents of almost all my friends were divorced or engaged in different stages of divorce proceedings. When Gilda played at my house she would sometimes be collected by her mother's lover, later her stepfather, to my own parents' consternation. It was not a situation they were used to, coming from a culture where the notion of step-parents was still unfamiliar since the children of divorced parents were usually entrusted to grandparents: all this is now changing with the collapse of the extended family.

Gilda had much to do with my Western education. One day, as

she and I were descending in the lift from her apartment, she hitched up her skirt, slipped off her pants and displayed herself to the uniformed Italian doorman. 'Tut, tut,' he said. 'You shouldn't do that, little girl.' At which she stuck out her tongue and ran out of the lift, twirling her pants and howling with laughter.

Sex became preoccupying in Indonesia where, on my father's appointment in 1969, I lived from the age of eleven to fourteen and attended an American Mission school in Djakarta. The hot, humid climate seemed to release the libido of the teenagers, who were only loosely disciplined by the motley collection of Western eccentrics, touched in one way or another by the confusions of the 1960s, who made up the teaching staff. Most appeared to have come to the tropics on some Conradian quest. It was a mad school. Everyone went barefoot. The mathematics teacher was an ex-Bronx taxi-driver who had done a stint on a kibbutz and had married a sexy black woman who taught us physical education.

Two of us were not allowed to join in the fun. For religious reasons I was forbidden to date, sit in the back of cars with boys or go to pyjama parties, and so was Magda, a girl from Warsaw whose father was at the Polish Embassy and who, for political reasons, could not fraternise with Americans. A Mormon girl, Cindy, wasn't supposed to have fun either but she did behind her parents' back, becoming the star of 'spin-the-bottle' games, a flimsy excuse for passionate petting.

My dilemma was that of a strictly brought up Muslim girl in a permissive school environment, a dilemma I see shared in Britain today by countless Asian girls whose families have been uprooted and brought to the West by political upheaval or economic necessity. They often rebel against restrictions much more forcefully than I chose to at the time.

There was, for example, the whole contentious question of PE. At its simplest, PE involved running and jumping, which in turn meant wearing the shortest of shorts. But in my Syrian childhood, well-brought-up girls did not run. I recall, as a ten-year-old in Damascus, dashing down the road to greet my teacher, only to be pulled up short by a stern rebuke: 'Aren't you ashamed to be running in the street?' Even less, of course, could a girl show her thighs. In Indonesia my mother was not happy when I wore the very short shorts required for games, with the result that I was eventually excused PE altogether and took refuge in the library. I was agreeably relieved because I didn't like undressing in front of other girls – at twelve I was already well developed – and in any event was still smarting from an incident which had happened earlier in the year.

Everyone was getting undressed in the games room. 'Hey, what's that?' a girl cried out, and all eyes were turned in my direction. Pinned to my bra was a cellophane envelope, half the size of a picture postcard, containing a piece of paper covered with small Arabic writing. 'Come on! Come on! Tell us what it is.' It was not something I could begin to explain. Like many Arab women, my mother had gone to a sheikh before leaving Damascus to request a talisman to protect me from ill-health. The holy man had written out some verses from the Qur'an on a piece of paper which, to preserve, my mother had folded up tightly and sealed in cellophane. I had worn it for so long that I had forgotten it was there. Every member of our family was so equipped. My father's talisman had frequently to be rescued from the washing machine, where it was thrown by mistake attached to some item of his clothing. 'It's a letter from my boyfriend in Syria,' I said finally, to head off my persecutors. I still blush at the lie.

At midday the students opened the lunch boxes which they had brought from home – chicken legs, peanut butter sandwiches and the like – and to my amazement would sometimes cry 'Yuck! I hate this stuff', and empty the box into the bin. Inwardly I would cry 'Haram! haram!', for I had been taught that throwing food away was criminal, and had never questioned it.

In that year I was chosen by our music teacher, Miss Murray, a missionary's daughter from Kansas, to star in the school musical, *The Music Man*. In the final scene the heroine and her travelling salesman lover sing a duet which ends in a kiss. There was the rub. My father would not allow it. 'We are Muslims,' he said. 'Such things are forbidden.' My understudy, an American girl, got the part instead. The irony was that when we all went to see the school production my father enjoyed it very much, and perhaps regretted his decision – although he never admitted it.

The point was that I was not allowed to have any contact with boys, and when one was brave enough to telephone me there were arguments at home for days afterwards. The only exceptions my parents would tolerate were an Egyptian whose family they knew and a Malaysian boy, son of the Malaysian ambassador – both of them Muslims. This was not because of fanaticism or xenophobia but because they supposed that these two youths would have had an upbringing similar to mine and would therefore not try anything on.

One day the Malaysian boy came in the chauffeur-driven embassy car to take me to a party given by Miss Murray, who had recently married Mr Bridges, our English teacher. But when I joined him in the back of the car my mother, for extra security, rushed out of the house, tapped on the car window and asked the boy to sit in front next to the chauffeur, which he did without demur.

We did not know that we were to be the only guests, or that Mr Bridges, an Englishman from Kent with a flair for teaching Shakespeare, had converted to Islam and had indeed persuaded Miss Murray to do so as well. In fact we had been invited because we were Muslims and the occasion was the *'Id*, the festival at the end of Ramadan. I had put on a miniskirt for the party, only to find that Miss Murray was more appropriately dressed as a Muslim woman in an ankle-length garment!

This whole Indonesian period – and indeed the New York

experience as well – was as much an education for my parents as for myself. They could see that I was caught between the values they had taught me and the life I saw around me at school, and for them too the transition from Islam to the West was a difficult one. When my sister, five years my junior, became an adolescent they had lived abroad a long time, had mellowed and relaxed, and were a good deal less protective.

I gradually became aware that the school curriculum in Indonesia presented as big a hurdle as the sexual mores of my peers. Geography was taught in terms of 'discovery' – the West discovering Africa or Asia or the Americas – with Columbus described in sentimental and heroic terms. When a Dutch girl who sat next to me learned where Syria was located on her map, she turned to me in real alarm: 'You come from *Asia!*'

Although Indonesia was a Third World and Muslim country we were taught white man's history – American and European wars, revolutions, triumphs. The rest of the world was either ignored or seen through the prism of Western superiority. Communism was the bogey of the classroom, an attitude shared by the students, as many of them were the children of American diplomats or Marine guards. But I came from Syria, a Muslim country on close terms with the Soviet Union. When we had to write a report on a country of our choice, I wrote mine about Russia and, to my teacher's annoyance, I did not portray it as an evil place.

Israel was the darling, and we were told to admire the Zionist success in conquering the barren desert. When I raised my hand to say that the Palestinians had been there first and had been driven from the fields they had planted, the teacher became very angry. 'You Arabs should forget about that,' she shouted. 'Countries that are winners get to keep what they win!' There was only one side to every issue, and it was not the side I was on.

*   *   *

Although I may have seemed a rebel in the Western setting of the Mission school in Djakarta, I had been affected more profoundly than I realised, as I was to discover on returning home to Syria in 1973. Aged fifteen, I was immediately crammed into a military uniform – for this was a Syria about to wage war on Israel – and subjected to the rigours of military training, including how to strip down, assemble and fire a Kalashnikov. Parading for hours in heavy army boots, I had reason to regret barefoot Indonesia. My instructors, fierce party cadres aflame with rural grievance, saw me as a soft Westernised bourgeoise on the wrong side of the political fence, and singled me out for rough treatment. As their ideological mission was to shape a 'new Syrian woman', they chose to make an example of me.

'Kabbani!' the instructor would holler over the microphone, 'Go at once to the lavatory and wet your hair.' She had decided that my short curls were the product of a hairdresser rather than of nature and needed, in the interest of military discipline, to be washed out. I was made to stand at attention in the middle of the parade ground with water trickling down my neck, waiting for my hair to dry. But the offending curls returned, and the next day I had to face the same abasement. In due course, every remaining trace of my Indonesian *dolce vita* was banished and a red lanyard appeared on my uniform, indicating an evolution from victim to victimiser: I became the instructor's assistant with special responsibility for ensuring that every girl's fingernails were short, clean and free from polish, that faces were innocent of make-up, and that no one was chewing gum.

This game-playing became serious when, on 6 October 1973, Syria and Egypt attacked Israel in a bid to regain the land Israel had seized in its 1967 aggression. Our whole building took to the cellar for fear of Israeli air raids, which came soon enough, with American-built Phantoms swooping low over our street and shattering our windowpanes. Three apartment blocks a little further down the road were totally obliterated by Israeli bombs, with great loss of civilian life.

Within a very few weeks of the outbreak of war, euphoria in Syria had turned to gloom. Differences arose between Damascus and Cairo, foreshadowing Sadat's later defection and his signing of the Camp David agreement. Henry Kissinger embarked on his mission to split the Arabs and protect Israel, a mission which was not yet apparent. He camouflaged his policy with the friendly business of renewing US diplomatic relations with Syria, broken in 1967. My father, a career diplomat, was chosen to be Syria's first ambassador in Washington, and so we packed our bags again for yet another foray into the Western world.

From my point of view the journey came at a decisive moment. In 1974 I was sixteen, I had passed my *baccalauréat*, and I was already on the marriage market. Every other day a prospective mother-in-law would telephone my mother asking to come and see me. I had a good many suitors – some known to me, others merely names – and was proud of the fact in much the same way as a girl in the West with lots of dates. Had we stayed in Syria, I might well have chosen one of them and settled into the comfortable arrangement of a marriage *à l'orientale*. Instead I was whisked away to an ambassador's residence in Washington and to the more dangerous environment of Georgetown University.

The paradox about Washington was that here, in the American capital, I learned to hate America. In Washington we as a family encountered a visceral antagonism to Arabs in general and to Syrians in particular, no doubt because of the extraordinary grip which Israel had on American imaginations. We found that our Middle East was viewed solely and exclusively through the medium of Israeli propaganda myths: that Israel was weak and the Arabs were strong; that Israel was in constant danger of annihilation; that it wanted peace and the Arabs did not; that its history was one of justice and of heroic settlement of the empty desert; that there was no such thing as Palestine or the Palestinians. There was no glimmering of understanding that it was the Arabs who were besieged, bombarded and driven from their homes by Israeli might, propped up by the United States.

It was not easy to live in an environment shaped by the deceit of our enemies. Every Arab believes that American policy towards the Middle East is made in Tel Aviv, but to discover that this was indeed the case, and not mere paranoia, was a great shock. Westerners can have little inkling of the rage and fear Arabs – and not only Arabs – experience when they realise that the world's greatest power has contempt for their aspirations. The attitude deeply ingrained in the American psyche is that Arabs or Iranians have absolutely no right to defend themselves. How dare they respond to Western aggression by using their 'oil weapon', by blowing up Marines, by taking hostages? I remember, some years later, Secretary of State George Shultz banging the table at one of his press conferences and declaring that no cause in the world justified the taking of American lives. That was all very well – might is right, the strong can forget about history – but how about Arab or Iranian lives sacrificed to Western strategic interests? And what about Palestinian and Lebanese lives taken so freely by Israel without a whisper of reproof from Washington – indeed, often with American complicity?

In Washington I became politicised. Military training in Syria and the experience of the October War had made me a crude but fiery nationalist, but now I began to grasp something of the problems faced by developing nations in a world still dominated by American power and by those countries, such as Israel, which had joined the winning side. I learned much of this on the Georgetown campus, then populated by a rich assortment of Arabs, Africans, Latin Americans, Iranians and Black Americans who, almost without exception, saw the world through the eyes of the underdog. We spent hours in discussion and it was brought home to me how similar were the dilemmas we faced, whatever the differences in our backgrounds. Of course there was always a minority of 'Third Worlders' among us anxious to embrace the American way of life – in other words, to assimilate. They despised us 'radicals' as we despised them.

It is not surprising that a Muslim upbringing includes a strong dose of anti-Westernism, given Western contempt for and ignorance about Islam. I was not wholly surprised when, at a graduate seminar at Georgetown, an American student asked me, 'How many wives does your father have? Do you live in a building or a tent and do you drive a camel or a car?' After the break-up of the Ottoman Empire in the First World War, Arabs suffered the daily presence of European colonialism and the humiliation profoundly marked them. When European power waned after the Second World War, it was replaced by an American-Israeli overlordship against which they are rebelling to this day.

Rummaging through an old trunk at my grandmother's house, I came upon a nationalist proclamation of the late 1920s:

> O Men of the Nation!
>
> Your women call on you to take up arms to protect your homes and your honour.
>
> Come and fight or the enemy will annihilate you together with your last hope of freedom.
>
> You will not be worthy of us unless you are ready to lay down your lives for your country, as your forebears did before you.
>
> Your nation will lend you strength and will pray for your victory.[10]

The occasion for this inflammatory document, signed by my grandmother, was an assault on a prayer leader in the Shaghur district of Damascus by three drunken French officers. They had forced him at gun point to interrupt the call to prayer and to come down from his minaret.[11] Emotion in the city ran high. Shopkeepers in the bazaar called an immediate strike and rolled down their metal shutters, a traditional form of protest.[12] Sensing the outrage of her guests at her regular 'at home' day, my grandmother called for pen and paper, and with the help of her aunt, a formidable woman who ran the Red Crescent charity, scribbled this call to arms, which she then read out to the assembled company. Those who could write made copies and pasted them up on walls on their way home.

In such ways women were swept into the nationalist movement. All too often their sons and husbands would be arrested for agitation and taken to prison. The women would cook for days and carry food to the prisoners. On some occasions black Senegalese soldiers, whom the French brought in to keep order and who inspired dread, would overturn their brass canteens and trample the food underfoot. Such oppression revived in Muslim breasts the old concept of *jihad*, of holy war against the invader. Little that has happened since has caused Muslims to feel otherwise towards the West.

Is the Western conscience not selective? The West feels sympathy for the Afghan Mujahedin, propped up by American intelligence just as the Nicaraguan Contras were, but feels no sympathy for militant Muslims who are not fighting its Cold War battles but have political concerns of their own. As I write, Palestinians are dying every day in the Occupied Territories – nearly 600 dead at the latest count, over 30,000 wounded and 20,000 in detention without trial – savage and prolonged curfews are imposed as routine collective punishments, homes are blown up, pregnant women gassed and beaten and unarmed boys kicked to death by regular soldiers, yet Israel remains a democracy in Western eyes, an outpost of Western civilisation. What is one to think of such double standards?

Considering these circumstances, it is not surprising that an extremist political Islam has taken root all over the world, fuelled by historical grievance, by poverty, by an overriding sense of powerlessness. The West bears more than a measure of responsibility for this phenomenon. For by interfering so forcefully in Muslim affairs, by overthrowing nationalist rulers (as was done in Iran, for example, in 1953) and setting up puppets in their place, by uncritical support for Israeli excesses, by milking Muslim resources and conspiring to keep the Muslim world economically, culturally and politically enthralled, the West has made us what we are: enraged and unforgiving.

6

OH, TO BE IN ENGLAND

In 1980 I was twenty-two. After a failed marriage in Beirut torn by civil war, I set my sights on a degree of Doctor of Philosophy from Cambridge University. I had worked and saved money for the undertaking, a place was promised me at Jesus College, and I had a subject: the image of the Orient, *my* Orient, as expressed in the novels, travel writing, scholarship and painting of Britain and France in the nineteenth century.

I had an idea that much of the misrepresentation and sheer dislike of the Muslim world which I had experienced in the United States and elsewhere had been shaped by a literary and artistic tradition which had flourished under the aegis of empire. In other words, culture and colonialism were intimately linked, with the former heavily influenced by the realities of power. When writers and painters saw the East as a place of violence and sex, of sloth and fanaticism, they were giving credence to the idea that Easterners were incapable of governing themselves and justifying and opening the way, however obliquely, for Europe's armies and colonial administrators. In particular, the image of Eastern women in the erotica of Richard Burton or as depicted in the work of a painter like Gérôme – naked slaves, courtesans reclining on Turkey carpets and the like – was, I believed, a construct of European imagination, bearing little relation to the truth and serving political rather than artistic ends.

I spent three years at Cambridge – a lot of my time in the Rare Books Room of University Library, perusing Victorian pornography

– and submitted my thesis (*Europe's Myths of Orient: Devise and Rule*[13]) to the Board of Graduate Studies in 1983. I then awaited the appointment of examiners by the Degree Committee of English, the governing body of the faculty to which I was attached.

In the early 1980s, the English faculty at Cambridge was at war with itself. Raymond Williams and Frank Kermode – 'grand old men' of humane left-wing leanings for whom the study of literature could not be separated from other disciplines which probed the social fabric – had come under attack from Christopher Ricks, a senior member of the English faculty, and other 'new Right' academics who took what seemed to me a more parochial view of English studies. A continental polymath like George Steiner, for example, with his erudition in half a dozen fields, offended against this Little England approach and went elsewhere.

Another target of the 'Thatcherites of Lit. Crit.' was Edward Said, Professor of English and Comparative Literature at Columbia, whose pioneering book *Orientalism*,[14] published in 1978, had argued that the West had 'invented' the East the better to control it. It was a book which had set me off on my own investigations. Said was much disliked by Cambridge conservatives for carrying literature into the field of politics – a taboo activity. The fact that he was a Palestinian scarcely helped matters.

One of Said's prominent critics was Richard Luckett, Fellow of Magdalene College and a specialist on seventeenth-century poetry, who had written a savage attack on *Orientalism* in the *Cambridge Quarterly*. Like all Orientals, Luckett had sneered, Said suffered from excessive emotionalism and was incapable of rational analysis. It was therefore with considerable trepidation that I learned that Christopher Ricks had put forward Richard Luckett's name to the Degree Committee as the 'internal' examiner of my thesis – precisely because of the views he had expressed about *Orientalism*. If Said had been savaged, what could I expect? I had a further reason for concern: not only was I an Arab writing in an anti-Western vein, but I was also a woman writing as a feminist at a time when Luckett himself, and Magdalene College as a whole, were known for their misogyny. I had some hopes in my 'external' examiner, the veteran historian of imperialism V. G. Kiernan, from Edinburgh University, whose book *The Lords of Human Kind*[15] could be read as a mild, anecdotal precursor of Said's.

My *viva voce* examination was held in a panelled room next to the chapel at Magdalene College, and my fears were not allayed when Mr Luckett greeted me with the words, 'Oh, you're white! We thought you would be black.' He soon made his position clear. My writing, he said, showed clear hatred of the West and did I really expect a Western university like Cambridge to reward me with a degree? Kiernan was more sympathetic but, missing the point of my argument, he confessed himself puzzled by my statement that Europeans had 'invented' Eastern eroticism. 'There *are* harems and captive women in them,' he chided. 'I saw them in India!' The upshot was that Luckett failed me and Kiernan passed me and, seeing that they could not persuade each other, appointed new examiners, and new ones after that, until no fewer than eight had read and reported on my work. It took three years of battling – as long again as my thesis had taken to write – for me to be awarded a doctorate.

During those three years of waiting, my whole life was in limbo and my disillusion with Cambridge University became pronounced. Was this an illustration of British 'fair play'? I was haunted by the ghost of a Sudanese student who, after five years of emotional and financial struggle to finish his dissertation, had been failed outright, whereupon, unable to face the humiliation of returning home empty-handed, he had committed suicide in his college room. Rightly or wrongly, I came to believe that it was the colour of his skin rather than the quality of his writing which his examiners had found unsatisfactory. Keenly aware of how close I myself had been brought to the abyss, I reached the conclusion that the three years I spent battling for my degree were more fruitful for my education than the years spent writing my thesis. I had been doctored by Cambridge all right, but not in the way I had expected.

This experience set me in violent confrontation with the system, not a satisfactory state of affairs. As chance would have it, at about this time I met a compatriot who had also been awarded a doctorate from a European university. He, however, had adopted a posture radically different from mine, although to my mind no more satisfactory: instead of confrontation, he had chosen assimilation.

Marwan came from a family similar to my own. We had known each other as adolescents in Damascus, and since his sister was a close friend of mine and our parents were distantly related, we had been allowed to socialise *en famille*. I then lost track of him for more than ten years.

Our reunion came at an exhilarating moment in my life. I had never been so free and would never be so free again: I was no longer a student and was earning my own living. I was unattached and living alone away from my country. I was travelling a great deal. I felt light and rootless. I had not yet made the identity choices which were later to shape me.

I arrived at Perpignan airport and looked about for the boy I had known. The man he had become was indistinguishable from the European holiday-makers who filled the arrival hall. He wore a sleeveless T-shirt and denim cut-offs, hardly the young dandy I remembered. His greetings in French were as casual as his clothes. I, on the other hand, in my best shoes and tailored suit, still the *jeune fille bien rangée* in his parents' salon, put out my hand to shake his and inquired after his health in Arabic.

I instantly sensed that I had made him uncomfortable, but only in retrospect did I fully understand why. He had done his best to sever ties to his family, to the country of his birth, to his language and to the Muslim faith in which he had been brought up. Anxious to distance himself from his background, he knew none of the several hundred Arab students who had studied with him at the University of Montpellier. France had become his permanent home and he could no longer envisage any other.

He had contracted a *mariage blanc* with a Frenchwoman in order to obtain the much-desired citizenship. He now called himself Mike. He had made a crucial psychological decision on which there was no turning back. To all intents and purposes he was now French.

At the time of our meeting he was involved with a divorced Frenchwoman of affluent bourgeois background, much older than himself, by whom he was about to have a child but to whom he found he could make no real commitment. Yet she was necessary to him, since through her he was able to fulfil what was clearly a psychological need to rebel against his family. He knew that his mother and father strongly disapproved of his arrangements, but this only strengthened his resolve to continue with them.

Marwan's parents were devout Muslims who found sexual transgressions difficult to comprehend, let alone forgive. No doubt they had hoped that their son would take a Muslim wife. Failing that, they expected him to marry his Frenchwoman. His refusal to do so was a social embarrassment which they felt bitterly, living as they did in a community where such things were unheard of. Like thousands of other young Muslim professionals from developing countries, Marwan had opted for life in the West, where beliefs they held sacred counted for nothing.

He soon broke the last link to his background when he decided to discontinue his annual visits home.

Was assimilation, I reflected, any better than the confrontation I had opted for? Not only did I disagree with his views, but I simply could not see how he had brought off such a total metamorphosis. Was there no middle way? Was it not possible to live in the West – and I mean really living, fully participating – without denaturing oneself as he had done? This was the puzzle which was to occupy me for some years, and I am still not sure that I have found a solution.

The Salman Rushdie affair has revived these questions for me. I could not fail to notice that some Muslim intellectuals of my acquaintance, living in England, felt compelled to attack Islam in order to move with the prevailing current of wholesale condemnation of Muslims. 'If you can't beat them, join them' seemed to be their philosophy. It was not a position I was inclined to adopt.

7

LA TRAHISON DES CLERCS

Some Westernised Muslim intellectuals have portrayed Salman Rushdie's brush with the Ayatollah as an example of the alleged incompatibility in Islam between the artist and the religious purist. The charge is that the authorities in Islamic countries do not tolerate artistic creativity or other free expressions of the human spirit. On this view, Rushdie was anathematised for his artistry, for his literary talent. This is one of the themes in *Iranian Nights*, the play rushed out by Tariq Ali and Howard Brenton in which, in one episode, the poet Omar Khayyam is confronted by the intransigence of the cleric.

Art and religion have certainly clashed in Islamic society, and continue to do so, but it is inaccurate to suggest that one has always triumphed over the other. The more common pattern is for them to coexist uneasily side by side, with first one then the other winning a round or two. For example, after the Iranian revolution there was an attempt by the clerics to shelve Iran's pre-Islamic artistic heritage, as well as post-Islamic but secular poets such as Omar Khayyam and Firdowsi. But there was great resistance from the Iranian public to these moves and they had to be softened, if not abandoned, in response to popular sentiment.[16]

The point may also be illustrated by the experience of my own family, which has produced two writers, a dramatist and a poet. Although separated by two generations, they both faced the outrage of the religious authorities but went on to win the contest in the end.

Abu Khalil al-Kabbani, the most distinguished of my creative ancestors, founded the first theatre in the Arab world in 1878 and is considered the father of Arab drama. In middle life he left a lucrative and respectable job to devote himself to writing and directing plays and even acting in them, a shocking undertaking at a time when actors were considered immoral. Unable to get women to perform on stage, he recruited young men to play the female parts, as was the practice in Elizabethan England. A self-taught linguist, he translated Shakespeare and Molière into Arabic and staged their works. As he was also a gifted musician and lyricist he wrote many scores and songs, which have entered the Arab musical repertoire, as well as numerous plays which he produced and directed himself. This activity won him an enthusiastic following among young people in Damascus, then a rigidly conservative city.

Not surprisingly, he aroused the wrath of the religious establishment, which accused him of corrupting the young. In defence of morality, the clerics incited youths to taunt him with obscenities, pelt him with rotten tomatoes and then with stones, and, in a grand finale, to set fire to his beloved theatre. Abu Khalil, who had bankrupted himself in building it, now found himself destitute. In great dejection he fled to Cairo, which he hoped would be a more liberal place. He rebuilt his playhouse – but again it was burnt down, this time at the urging of Egyptian sheikhs. The irony was that Abu Khalil was a pious man who never wrote anything blasphemous or even frivolous. His plays were high-minded works glorifying Islamic history. He returned to Damascus, sick and broken, and shortly afterwards, in 1902, died of a fever. Today both Cairo and Damascus honour his memory, and Syria has given his name to its leading theatre.

As a small child my grandmother witnessed the old man's humiliating end, but grew up to see his reputation restored. She was therefore prepared to handle another conflict between art and religion involving a member of her family – this time her own son.

In 1940, when he was seventeen, her son Nizar Kabbani – my

uncle – came and asked her for 300 liras, a small fortune at the time. Taken aback, she wanted to know why. He confessed that he had secretly written a long poem and wanted to have it published. Although my grandmother was unable to read, like so many women of her generation, she was intelligent and had a natural admiration for art. She slipped a heavy gold bracelet off her wrist and handed it to him. 'Sell this to the Jewish jeweller round the corner and you will get what you need.'

Soon afterwards, Nizar's book appeared in the few bookshops of the city. It had a bold cover showing a dancing girl, drawn by an artist friend, and a suggestive title: *Samba*. But its contents were still more inflammatory – one of the first erotic poems written in modern Arab literature, and its author hardly more than a boy!

A day or two later, quite unaware of this development, my grandfather, walking home from work, was accosted by a group of enraged clerics. 'Have you no shame, brother, to allow this filth to come out of your house?' one of them thundered. Tawfiq Kabbani was a pillar of the community, a nationalist, and the proud owner of a chocolate and nougat factory. He suddenly found a book thrust into his face with his son's name printed across the gaudy cover. Pulling off his belt, he cracked it in the air as if to show that his son would get a thrashing, and stormed home.

News of his encounter with the clerics had preceded him. Anticipating trouble, my grandmother had sent Nizar to her sister's house with instructions to stay there until morning.

'Faiza!' my grandfather bellowed. 'Where is that no-good son of yours? Why am I the last to know what goes on in this house?' Marching into the sitting-room, he slammed the door and settled down to read his son's work. At dinner that night he ate in silence. He then went upstairs to wash and pray, put on his best suit, donned his fez, and went to the Mosque to tell the sheikhs not to meddle in his affairs: in his view his son's poems were not offensive to God.

Today, my Uncle Nizar is perhaps the most popular Arab poet, but he also has the distinction of being banned in half the Arab world.

I do not consider the Rushdie affair as a struggle between creativity and religious obscurantism. In fact, because of the nature of Rushdie's attack on Islam, it has become almost impossible for a devout Muslim to see his book as a novel at all (no doubt another irony of this affair). It is almost beside the point to say that Muslim readers have failed to appreciate his artistry (I for one have long admired his art, but still found in *The Satanic Verses* such a negative political message that it killed my reading of it as a novel).

That Salman Rushdie is a gifted novelist I have not the least doubt. I shall never forget my excitement on reading *Midnight's Children*, which revealed to me the possibility of satisfying simultaneously the Booker Prize audience, which requires a literary reading of the text, and the audience which demands a political message. The pioneering achievement of this novel was to advance cultural accommodation by ingeniously managing to make the English language accurately express what had been until then an untranslateable actuality, a world hitherto unknown in the West. In my reading, *Midnight's Children* was no exotic fable; it was a precise description of the complicated political reality I belong to.

This novel, which made Salman Rushdie famous, won him a double following, satisfying Western as well as non-Western readers – something which *The Satanic Verses* has signally failed to do. Its failure is due to the fact that the aesthetic form of the book and its political message, which were inseparable in *Midnight's Children*, have broken loose from each other, each part taking its readership, both boiling with outrage. *The Satanic Verses* seems to concern itself only with satisfying Western literary values, which inevitably leads to a recanting of its author's political stance. Its 'tone' does not translate across cultures. Although there is a long and lively tradition of satirical writing in Islam, the fact that the novel was read by Muslims not as a serious critique but as frivolous mockery reveals to me how wide the gulf has grown between Rushdie and his origins, a charge he would forcefully deny. It also reveals that he is now writing for Western sensibilities and, in so doing, disregarding Muslim sensibilities completely.

According to the 'literary' apprehension of a text, an author is allowed unlimited licence, whereas a more *engagé* reading will insist on political relevance and political responsibility. In Western 'high culture', literature is too often supposed to enjoy the privilege of rising above the 'crudities' of politics – a stance which denies literature any real political significance. But for non-Western readers, the notion of a literary text which is also political is much more familiar.

Such a view of literature is condemned by certain circles in the West as both tyrannical (bordering on Stalinism) and primitive, a simplistic interpretation of fiction as untransformed politics. However, those who consider a political reading of a text reductive do so because they have an investment in an evaluation which holds only certain experiences to be valid. This is in itself a political – not to say reactionary – judgement, although they would not necessarily like to admit it. What this is really saying, to put it bluntly, is that only white Western patriarchy and the tradition it has established are to be respected. Along with the self-assertion of other cultures, the politically charged creative writing of feminists has also earned some dismissive scorn.

When a writer from the margins breaks into the big time, there is a sense of exhilaration that he or she has overcome formidable obstacles. Such writers, suddenly famous, are beguiled into believing that inclusion in the cultural establishment has been secured on their own terms. This is a delusion. Allowed freedom to manoeuvre to begin with, the writer as time passes will be hedged in, unwittingly depoliticised and by extension compromised – a paranoid view, you may think, but one that is justified by an examination of the workings of cultural politics. So when Muslims allege that there is a conspiracy behind *The Satanic Verses*, they are giving crude but not totally absurd expression to their response to a complex cultural reality.

Crossing cultures is necessarily a problem, even a danger, for writers. Success erodes in the author the sense of original identity – indeed, almost comes to replace that identity. Authors are of course aware of the problem and even accept the process, in the high-minded hope that cultural divisions will be transcended. All too often, however, success presupposes (or rewards) rejection of one's roots. Rushdie's (perhaps unwitting) decision in *The Satanic Verses* to recant a political project that he had been identified with, to go back on what he had stood for, seems to me an unfortunate consequence of his success, which may have led him to feel that he is no longer accountable to his non-Western readership.

Accountability is not tyranny or meddling with the artistic process; it is a duty writers owe to their readers and their background. Writers who lose sight of accountability risk becoming self-indulgent and politically irresponsible. Their position as 'privileged insiders', with unique insight into their own communities, gives them an authority and credibility that no outsider has. The danger is that their texts may be read as truths. For example, women celebrities who attack feminism are presumed to know what they are talking about because they are women, and are therefore apt to be taken seriously.

In much the same way, and although he is a gifted writer, V. S. Naipaul's writings about the India of his ancestors demonstrate his alienation from it and his distaste for it. They show his identification with a sanitised West, which in turn receives his testimony as the plain truth. I fear that the same phenomenon may be happening with Rushdie.

There is a luxury of intellectual despair in which some authors wallow as soon as they can afford to. Life is seen with unrelieved political pessimism; there is no hope of change or transformation. The only reasonable responses to this are doubt and a conviction of futility. Nothing is hallowed, nothing is revered, belief in anything is ridiculed – belief in God and in the goodness in humanity most of all. This is the dispirited view taken by much Modernist writing. Salman Rushdie himself places *The Satanic Verses* firmly in this Modernist tradition.[17]

Yet there are other ways of seeing the world. Many writers, worldwide, would strongly repudiate so defeatist an account of experience, which may strike them as a denial of life's power to regenerate. Unless one continues to insist that the world is transformable, one is destined to remain victimised by it. Arthur Miller, in *After the Fall*, reminds us that we have somehow to forgive and rise above our murderous past, if we are to survive morally in a post-Holocaust universe.

Indeed, it is time we transcended our history. In this interdependent world, confrontation must be condemned as obsolete for its many unacceptable meanings. It means declaring war on the 'Other', denying them legitimacy, denigrating them, dehumanising them. But assimilation is not the answer either, since that easily becomes a form of inverted racism, accepting that one culture is superior to another.

Much as I admire Salman Rushdie as a writer, I cannot begin to applaud *The Satanic Verses*. I feel that it has added dramatically to the clash of cultures, to a confrontationalism at once self-defeating and damaging. Saddest of all, I feel that this book has set back the cause of anti-racism, to which Rushdie himself has over the years been so eloquent a contributor.

REFERENCES

1. Fay Weldon, *Sacred Cows*, Chatto, London, 1989, pp. 6, 12, 29–30.
2. Conor Cruise O'Brien, *The Times*, 11 May 1989.
3. I am deeply indebted to the work of Norman Daniel, *Islam and the West: The Making of an Image*, Edinburgh, 1960; and R. W. Southern, *Western Views of Islam in the Middle Ages*, Cambridge, MA, 1980.
4. See Maxime Rodinson, *Europe and the Mystique of Islam*, I. B. Tauris, London, 1988.
5. Muhammad Husayn Haykal, *The Life of Muhammad*, North American Trust Publications, Washington, DC, 1976.
6. Alan Pike, 'Rushdie Affair Lifts the Lid on Long-standing Racial Tensions', *Financial Times*, 24 June 1989.
7. The *People*, 11 June 1989.
8. Dr Shabbir Akhtar, *Guardian*, 27 February 1989.
9. Marina Warner addressing the Institute of Contemporary Arts, London, 19 March 1989; text in Lisa Appignanesi and Sara Maitland (eds), *The Rushdie File*, Fourth Estate, London, 1989, p. 208.
10. Ghazzi family papers, n.d. (*c.* 1929).
11. This story is recounted by the Syrian writer Dr 'Abd al-Salam al-Ujayli, in *An-Naqid*, January 1989.
12. Philip Khoury, *Syria and the French Mandate: The Politics of Arab Nationalism, 1920–1945*, I. B. Tauris, London, 1987.
13. Rana Kabbani, *Europe's Myths of Orient: Devise and Rule*, Macmillan Press Ltd, 1986; paperback edn Pandora Press, London, 1988.
14. Edward Said, *Orientalism*, Routledge & Kegan Paul, London, 1978.
15. V. G. Kiernan, *The Lords of Human Kind: European Attitudes towards the Outside World in the Imperial Age*, London, 1969.
16. Shireen Hunter, 'Islam in Power: The Case of Iran', in Shireen

Hunter (ed.), *The Politics of Islamic Revivalism: Diversity and Unity*, Center for Strategic and International Studies, Washington, DC, 1988, p. 270.

17. Interview with Salman Rushdie, 27 January 1989, by 'Bandung File', broadcast 14 February 1989 on Channel 4.